5%MORE

MAKING SMALL CHANGES

5%MORE

TO ACHIEVE
EXTRAORDINARY
RESULTS

MICHAEL ALDEN

WILEY

Published by John Wiley & Sons, Inc., Hoboken, New Jersey.
Published simultaneously in Canada.

For general information about our other products and services, please contact our Customer Care Department within the United States at (800) 762-2974, outside the United States at (317) 572-3993 or fax (317) 572-4002.

Wiley publishes in a variety of print and electronic formats and by print-on-demand. Some material included with standard print versions of this book may not be included in e-books or in print-on-demand. If this book refers to media such as a CD or DVD that is not included in the version you purchased, you may download this material at http://booksupport.wiley.com. For more information about Wiley products, visit www.wiley.com.

Library of Congress Cataloging-in-Publication Data:

Names: Alden, Michael, 1975- author.
Title: 5% more : making small changes to achieve extraordinary results / Mike Alden.
Other titles: Five percent more
Description: Hoboken, New Jersey : John Wiley & Sons, Inc., [2016] | Includes
  index.
Identifiers: LCCN 2016016538 (print) | LCCN 2016026080 (ebook) |
  ISBN 978-1-119-28186-3 (cloth) | ISBN 978-1-119-28187-0 (pdf) |
  ISBN 978-1-119-28188-7 (epub)
Subjects: LCSH: Motivation (Psychology) | Performance. | Success.
Classification: LCC BF503 .A48 2016 (print) | LCC BF503 (ebook) | DDC
  650.1—dc23
LC record available at https://lccn.loc.gov/2016016538

Printed in the United States of America

10 9 8 7 6 5 4 3 2 1

This book is dedicated to my beautiful, smart, athletic, amazing little girl, Morgan. You make Daddy so proud every day. I love you to the moon and back.

Contents

SECTION V 5 Percent Compounded

Acknowledgments

I would first like to acknowledge my beautiful girlfriend, Shauna. They say behind every great man there is a great woman. I don't know if I'm a great man, but I have a great woman beside me, behind me, and all around me. If it weren't for her hard work, dedication, and ability to deal with my craziness, I would not be the person I am today. When describing our relationship, many times I sum it up to "she gets me." But in all reality, we get each other, and that's what makes it work. Thank you, Babe! I love you!

Next, I would like to acknowledge my team at Blue Vase Marketing. There are a lot of great companies out there, and what I have found is that they are great because of the people who help build them. The people who took a chance on me early—Chris, Jason, Shauna—I cannot thank you enough. There are so many more people who make up Blue Vase and you know who you are. Your hard work, unwavering dedication, and loyalty have allowed me to write this book. Thank you!

I want to also thank my editor, friend, and confidant Chris Benguhe. I knew nothing about being an author or really how to properly write a book. Chris has guided me, counseled me, and, many times, just listened to me rant about the process. From the beginnings in my first book to this book, Chris has always been there. So, when you get to the meat of the book, if things sound just a little bit better, it is because Chris pushed me 5 Percent More, but, more important, he gave more and made this book what it is today.

I would be remiss if I did not mention Larry Benet. Larry has introduced me to influential people in the business world whom I would not have met if it hadn't been for him. More specifically,

Larry's introduction to John Wiley & Sons has allowed this book to be published by one of the biggest publishers in the world. Thank you, Larry!

Last, I want to thank my mom and dad. It is a bit of a cliché to thank Mom and Dad, but if it weren't for moms and dads, we wouldn't be here. Both my mom and my dad have given me advice, a shoulder to cry on, and, more important, encouragement along the way. Thank you, Mom and Dad. I love you both very, very much!

Introduction

After my first national best-selling book *Ask More, Get More*, I received some fantastic feedback and accolades. But, when I had an opportunity to sit down and talk with people about achieving their goals, I found that most people, from all walks of life, still want more.

They want more money; they want to be able to take their family on vacation; they want more freedom; and they want to be healthier, both physically and mentally.

Ultimately, they want a better quality of life for themselves and their family.

Some of those I met told me that they had read every self-help or personal development book they could get their hands on. They believed in all of the "principles" in my book and the thousands of other books out there. They listened to motivational speakers on their way to work; they listened to motivational speakers at the gym; they went to seminars. They did everything they were supposed to do. When you talked with most of these people I am referring to, they were also upbeat and positive people. But, despite all of the time and money they put in on "personal development," they were not where they wanted to be. Some were not only not where they wanted to be, but they were actually in a worse situation than they had been before any sort of "self-help" program.

Why is that? Is "self-help" a farce? Can the power of positive thinking actually work, or is it just something that's powerful sounding but doesn't actually ring true in real life? There are so many people who spend their hard-earned money on trainings, books, audios, and seminars every year. Why aren't all of these people wildly successful? Why haven't they been able to achieve their goals? Where is the disconnect?

And what about the people who don't read self-help books? What about your average, everyday American? Why are so many people stuck? Is there something that the average, everyday person can do to get ahead? And is that something that is truly achievable, something that doesn't cost money, something that yields real tangible results?

In 5% More, I will attempt to answer why so many people "fail." I will try to show that there is a connection between one's thoughts, between one's dreams, between one's goals, and their actions. Like in my book Ask More, Get More, you will find that the answers to some of the above questions seem ridiculously simple and easy to answer, and you will also find that taking action is easy and that anyone can do it.

In fact, I will not even make you wait to read the whole book to find out the ultimate answer. I will give it to you right here in the introduction to this book, in the very first few pages.

If you just give 5 Percent More effort in any aspect of your life, you will not only achieve your goals, you will surpass them.

If you are curious and want me to substantiate the last sentence, then read on. I promise this book will give you more than you ever imagined: a look at how we can dramatically change our lives by adding just 5 Percent More effort. Most people are looking for a way to improve their health, maximize their wealth, and obtain more wisdom, but most have trouble achieving their goals. Well, 5 Percent More is a way for any person of any age, any background, anywhere in the world to improve his life and achieve his goals just by adding 5 Percent More effort. How is this possible? How can a book with such a simple premise accomplish so much?

Well, let me give you a little background on where and how 5 Percent More became a reality for me. I was in a spinning class and totally exhausted, counting the seconds and minutes to the end of the class, and the instructor said that she wanted 5 Percent More out of us. She said that this next 5 percent is what really makes the class, that this next 5 percent burns more fat than the previous 40 minutes in the class, and that this 5 Percent More effort will have an impact on our metabolism hours after we get out of the class. She said 5 Percent More effort will get you an infinite amount more out of your body. When you are that exhausted and being pushed to the limit, you have to trust what they are saying and just push through. I noticed that not one person stopped, not one person even slowed down. We were all different sizes, shapes, ages, and personalities but we all trusted what she said, and we *all* gave at least 5 Percent More. In fact, most gave a lot more than that. It was interesting to me that all she asked for was 5 Percent More, yet it was obvious most gave more and maintained it throughout the last five minutes. She was onto something.

As I sat there afterward, half dead on the spin bike, I began to reflect on what would happen if we applied just 5 Percent More to virtually every aspect of our lives. Was there research out there that showed what 5 Percent More can do in virtually every aspect of your life? I didn't have the answer right then and there, but I began to study what our lives would look like if we had or did or wanted just 5 Percent More. The information I found and the science to support what just a little effort can do in virtually every aspect of your life was compelling. But when I dug a little deeper into my own life and the lives of others who have been successful for anecdotal evidence, it was even more astounding and profound.

In this book, I will discuss some of the science, some of the psychology, and even more of the common sense behind 5 Percent More and how that applies to your life—from just being 5 percent faster as an athlete to 5 percent smarter as a student to being 5 percent healthier than the average person, to improving your business by being 5 Percent More efficient or improving your sales by just 5 percent. It is truly amazing how something as simple as just 5 Percent More can have dramatic life-altering changes in your life.

Chapters range from discussing what 5 Percent More would do for an Olympic athlete, to what reading more to our children would do, and even how a slight increase in one's belief level in whatever one is doing can have dramatic results.

What I hope will really make this book stand out to you is that, while so many others try to cast a wide net by claiming that "everyone" should read a particular book, I believe that *5% More* truly is a book everyone will *want* to read. Maybe you have read all the other self-help books and nothing changed in your life, or maybe you're looking for answers to get you to the next level. That is precisely why I wrote *5% More.*

I don't claim to be a self-help expert—but I am an expert student of success, and I have found that almost everybody wants more. More happiness, better health, more financial stability, more discipline, and just a better life. But most if not all of the "self-help" books and programs fail to recognize that, although most people want more, the techniques, strategies, and theories work for only a small percentage of people, thus leaving a majority of people behind. So why would you want to read another "self-help" or "personal transformation" book?

People from all walks of life are struggling to make ends meet; people are having a tough time providing basic necessities for their families. Children are faced with competitive challenges as early as kindergarten, and even they want more. If you are high school athlete looking to get an athletic scholarship, a concerned parent, a business owner looking for a way to improve your bottom line, then look no further. The simple secrets in *5% More*, revealed through its inspiring stories, interviews, and research, proves that all most people need is just 5 Percent More to get what they want.

The Philosophy of 5 Percent More

CHAPTER 1

How to Give 5 Percent More—or Less

Asking for 5 Percent More and not following up with action won't work. Dreaming about being 5 percent richer, or your kids being 5 percent higher in their class, or being 5 percent smarter doesn't just happen. I always tell people that dreams are for sleeping. Goals are for achieving. And you achieve your goals only by taking action.

Since my last book, I have had a lot of my close friends confide in me that they wanted to do something, or that they had a goal or an idea but never did anything about it. One of those friends whom I grew up with is named Lonnie. When I lived in the projects, we lived in a duplex; I lived in 13 and he lived in 11. Over the years, we have stayed in contact. He made a great life for himself and his family: he has a beautiful wife, two beautiful kids, a great house, great job, a boat, and many other material things. One day while talking about what I have accomplished and built through my business, he said that he "wanted to do something, wanted to make something, wanted to do something great." Well, Lonnie is one of the handiest guys I know. He can fix and pretty much build anything. So one day while he was working in his yard hauling things from his back yard to the front yard, mostly leaves and other debris, he came up with an ingenious way to move that type of stuff quickly, efficiently, and effortlessly. He came to me and showed it to me; then he created some videos showing the utility of it, came up with a name for it, and was just so excited about it. So I asked him, "What are you going to do with it?" He looked at me with his head down and said, "I know I should do something, but I don't know." I said, "Lonnie, you have been thinking about doing 'greater things'; you have been thinking about your invention for months; you actually created a prototype. So now, why not take it to the next level?" He was still hesitant, until I reminded him of the story about the older guy who should've, could've, or would've, if only he did. His time had passed and now he was sitting on his porch telling his grandkids about how great he could have been if he had only followed through on the thought he had. He would have built an empire; buildings would have been named after him; he would have every material thing any man could want; but he didn't. We all know this guy, the "if I had only" guy. Those guys are the ones who let societal norms and negative influences destroy their aspirations. It's a sad thing, and I did not want to see this happen to my good friend Lonnie.

So Lonnie took the next step. He had mechanical drawings done of his invention, he hired a patent attorney, and he is in the process of making his invention a reality. Now, could this flop? Sure, but he will never know if he doesn't give it a shot. This idea and the creation of it have not cost Lonnie a lot of money. But, through his thoughts and his physical manifestations of those thoughts with action, he now has a patent pending. That is an accomplishment in and of itself.

AN IDEA WITHOUT A PLAN IS JUST AN IDEA

We have all heard the above axiom. We have all had a great "idea" but never followed through with it. We have all met the "if I had only" guy who also had a bunch of ideas. Many times, a person's ideas or dreams are not realistic and should just remain what they were. But what I have found in business and in life is that what separates the successful from the unsuccessful people is the determination to implement their ideas. This is a small part of the grand plan of building a brand, or turning an idea into a reality, but it is a key element of any type of success. If you truly believe in your idea and you have done the legwork to determine that your idea should become a reality, then you must implement your idea. You must take that small step like Lonnie did, which is turning his idea into a reality. I'm not talking about turning dreams into reality; I'm talking about taking a viable idea and turning it into a reality. See, Lonnie's idea actually has utility; there is a need for it. There are other things that try to accomplish the same goal, but he just figured out a better way of doing it. Implementation of your idea is critical for success, and most people don't know how to do it. You will find the answers as you read on, and they are very simple.

In order to actually get 5 Percent More, you need to take action. We are talking about only 5 percent, and in many circumstances even less than 5 percent. I'm not telling you to radically change your life and your daily habits, because I will show that dramatic changes don't work long term. It just takes 5 Percent More action.

When people ask me about how to take action, I break it down to two things. Thoughts + Physical Activity = Action. Thoughts are not dreams. What I mean by thoughts is actually seeing yourself making 5 Percent More money or whatever the goal is, and also thinking about how you will do it. In a way, it is three things: seeing it, thinking about it, and doing it. Now, I can't show *you* exactly how to make money at your particular job or livelihood in this book. But *you* know what you can do to start taking action in order to accomplish that. So, begin to mentally take action. Then combine that mental action with physical activity.

Let me give you an example in the area of physical fitness. Let's say you want to want to lose weight, and for simplicity let's say you want to lose 5 percent of your overall body weight. Let's also assume you are a 200-pound man. Let's also assume that you exercise, maybe 30 minutes a day, 3 days a week. All I am advocating for is to add 4.5 minutes more at a 5 Percent More intensity level. But even before that, I need you to think about and visualize what that means. If you are like me and do spinning a few times a week, then go 5 percent harder 5 Percent More of the time.

Now for all of the physical trainers and fitness buffs out there, my example may not necessarily yield 5 percent reduction in body weight; this is just an example for people to understand what Action really is. But combine the above with a 5 percent reduction in calories, and a 5 percent overall weight loss will certainly happen. Later on, we will discuss 5 percent compounded and how adding or just reducing 5 percent of practically any aspect of your life will yield unimaginable results.

So if you are dreaming about something, I want you to modify your dreams and turn them into goals—tangible, quantifiable objectives that can be measured. Then take Action. Mentally see yourself achieving your goal; mentally map out or devise a plan to achieve your goal; then take physical action. Where does the 5 percent play a role here? Spend 5 percent of your day working toward your goal. Just 5 Percent More effort and action. Again, just so I'm clear, it's mental *and* physical action. So the modified formula really looks like this: Seeing your goal + thinking about how to achieve your goal + physical activity = Action.

To further drive home this point about Action: If you are doing nothing with your life, if you are sitting home watching television waiting for something to happen but realizing you will not achieve anything by continuing this behavior, start by taking 5 percent of your day and work toward a goal. Now, 5 percent of the total day is only 72 minutes, but if you take waking hours it's even less, like 35 to 40 minutes. If your goal is to get off the couch and become a productive citizen, then take action, just a little each day in the beginning, to get to where you want to be. Too many people dive into something 100 percent and lose steam. If your habits have been that of a lazy person on the couch, then radically changing your day is unrealistic and a recipe for failure. Modify or change your actions to something that is going to get you to your goal by allotting just 5 percent of your time to get there.

Now, this doesn't just apply for those who are downright lazy and doing nothing, it applies to everyone in every scenario or situation imaginable. If you are a busy working mom with three kids and want to further your education, but can never seem to find the time, simply take 5 percent of the time you do have to achieve your goal. The great news is, with the proliferation of online degrees, your travel time is now zero. You can literally take classes in your bed. Many of these online schools are super-flexible, and you take the classes based on your schedule.

The 5 Percent More philosophy also applies to those who are looking to get to the top of their career path or goal. It may be the vice president of an organization who wants to become the president of his division, a Team Leader who wants to become a manager, or a worker in a factory who wants to be the foreman. Everyone at the top or the pinnacle of success in virtually every industry does more than the rest, and that is what separates society. The people who do just a little bit more, who work just a little bit harder, who spend just a little bit more time, who prepare just a little bit more, achieve greatness. Take it from someone who struggled his whole life to get ahead, from education to business. I realized that in order to get ahead, in order to become the businessperson I am today, I needed to put in just a little bit more effort. Some would argue I put in way more effort than 5 percent. Some would argue I was and am obsessed with being successful in all that I do. They may be right, but it all starts with 5 Percent More action. Then it snowballs to what I call compounded 5 Percent More, so that 5 percent last month becomes 50 percent now.

As I discussed in the introduction to this book, when I was in a spin class exhausted and wanting to just get off the bike, I realized

I could do 5 Percent More, I could push myself 5 percent harder and longer. As I looked around the room, as I said earlier, I saw everyone else could as well. But only a few could do 50 Percent More, and those were the people who had, at some point, started with just 5 Percent More.

5 Percent More means 5 Percent More effort, 5 Percent More dedication, 5 Percent More commitment and you can change your world beyond what you thought was possible. Come with me on this journey one step at a time, as I share many of the stories and anecdotes from my own life. All I ask is that every step of the way you open your mind 5 Percent More.

TAKE THEM AS FAR AS THEY CAN SEE, THEN THEY WILL SEE FURTHER

I learned that phrase from an unethical, nefarious businessman who is now in jail for his wicked ways. This man achieved what appeared to be supreme success; he had homes all over the world, he drove cars that cost more than most people's homes, he dined at the finest restaurants, wore clothes from the finest designers, and had more money than he knew what to do with. Why would I share this phrase from such an unscrupulous character? Well, the phrase is not evil and neither is its meaning. But it is very powerful when you want to achieve something, whether it is jogging to the next telephone pole or one more lap around the track, or one more sale before the end of the day. Once you get there, just ask for 5 Percent More effort out of yourself. You have already achieved your goal, so you have nothing to lose. You only have things to gain. Now imagine if you did this every day in every aspect of your life. Take yourself as far as you can see, then once you get there take yourself just 5 percent further.

Why did that unscrupulous businessperson end up in jail and lose everything? He appeared to have given more effort, he appeared to try just a little bit more than others, but what he was really doing was cheating. He was certainly 5 percent better at cheating, which gave him temporary success, but it ultimately led to his demise. You see, he told people that he would take them as far as they could see and they would then see further, but what they eventually did was fall off a cliff after he got all he could out of them.

If you are 5 percent better at cheating, stealing, or committing fraud, you will eventually end up broke and in jail. You see, 5 Percent More works virtually for everything, including dubious activity, so you must be careful when applying what you have learned so that it is for good and ethical purposes. Fast success never lasts. But if you use 5 Percent More for good ends, it can help you to achieve anything good. It did for me.

Now, I'm a marketing guy. I sell products on television. Yeah, they are infomercials. It's not the only thing my company does, but it's what we are really good at. Plus, we sell mostly supplements on television, which adds a layer of skepticism. There are companies every year in my industry that get sued or shut down for being 5 percent better at cheating or lying or defrauding the public. Some people will always look down upon what we do as a company. My company, Blue Vase Marketing, prides itself in being the best at what we do. That means we are better in every aspect of the business, including compliance. Are we perfect? No. Do we make mistakes? Yes. Why am I telling you this? Sometimes, as individuals, we look at others from the outside and judge. I don't blame those people. However, if you are one of those people, suspend your judgment and read the book. What I'm discussing, and have discovered, has propelled me to levels that not only seemed unattainable to most, but downright unrealistic and preposterous to even think about. I was and am a kid from the projects who grew up around poverty and despair and learned how simple concepts like 5 Percent More could get me more than most. If that's you, then let's get real and learn from someone who should have nothing but has more than most, from financial freedom to material things people usually dream about.

HIGH SCHOOL HERO TO COLLEGE ZERO—WHAT DOES IT TAKE TO BE A STAR?

In my book *Ask More, Get More*, I discussed tidbits of my past and how I grew up in order to illustrate how I had many obstacles and struggles as well as many accomplishments. But what even I didn't realize when I wrote it was that so much of how my success came about had to do with the 5 Percent More concept, although I didn't realize it at the time. When I achieved great things it was usually because I was applying the principle. When I didn't, it was usually because I was stagnating, unable to see the importance of 5 Percent More. Sometimes it was because I was doing everything *but* 5 Percent More.

One major accomplishment in my youth was being accepted to college. In 1993, I was fortunate enough to be accepted to Springfield College in Springfield, Massachusetts, a small college with a primary focus on physical education and athletic training, but it had a decent liberal arts school as well. They had a political science program, which is what I was interested in. I remember feeling a little uneasy and nervous my first few days in college, somewhat like a fish out of water, a kid from the projects who still had a chip on his shoulder and was now in a setting that was unfamiliar. I was, in essence, alone and left to my own devices, left to try to figure out how I was going to make my way there and in the world in general. Like many students, there was certainly an adjustment period with relation to basic things such as time management of the day-to-day activities. I was on the football team so I was able to be a part of a group, which was somewhat comforting.

This is where I really began to realize that small things such as your GPA or your 40-yard dash time or your vertical leap can have a dramatic impact on your athletic and academic career. I remember being on campus one day with just the football team and meeting with the football coaches and becoming acutely aware of how small things have a huge impact. We were getting our body fat measured, height, vertical jump, and a few other things. I was waiting in line and it was my turn to have my height measured. The coach asked me how tall I was, and I said I was six foot one inch. He didn't say anything. Then he measured my height. Apparently according to him I was six feet. He then looked at me and said if I was six foot one I wouldn't be playing at Springfield College and would be playing for a bigger program. One inch? Really? Well, except for a few outliers in athletics, small things such as your height do impact your future. Well, I can't control my height, but other things—such as body fat, vertical jump, and 40-yard dash—are all things I could change or improve upon. During that same time, one coach sat me down after taking my body fat and told me that I was essentially carrying around 20 pounds of fat and I needed to improve my body fat if I wanted to play on the team. Now, I thought I was in decent shape, but when you look at college athletes, especially the elite ones, I was practically obese.

I never became a star football player but I got on the field, and every year I played a little bit more because of things like improving my 40-yard dash from a 5.0 to a 4.75 or my bench press from a one rep max of 315 to a three rep max of 365. Now, though it was true that the guys who really had success on the field had a whole lot of natural talent (as did I), quite frankly, they worked just a little bit harder than me in the off season, in the weight room, and nutritionally. I worked hard, but just hard enough to stay on the team and get a little playing time, not hard enough to be a little bit faster and stronger. Instead of always trying to give 5 Percent More as they were, I was focused only on those simple goals, and then once I attained them, I lost interest in giving more effort. I can't tell you why, but I can tell you that I was very unhappy on the football team. I remember making excuses and blaming my lack of playing time on things like the performance-enhancing drugs some of the guys were taking, but my unhappiness was due to me just not working hard enough. In high school, I was able to dominate due to my size and natural speed and didn't really work that hard at it, but when you climb up to the next level, in order to have success you need to try harder. It really doesn't take *a lot* more effort or time, just a little bit more.

For instance, if at Springfield I had been able to get my speed to a 4.6, without question I would have been starting. Just a small percentage decrease in my speed would have certainly ensured me a starting spot. Some would argue that it would take a lot of work to get my time down that low, and they would be right if I were an unfit slob, but I was a college athlete and just needed to make some small changes to get better. Even if I didn't get to that 4.6 (which, by the way, I was clocked at a couple times, just not consistently), the coaching staff would have taken notice and probably given me more opportunity.

The guys on the team who got the most attention were the ones who, at the end of the day, worked harder; it's that simple. Some worked harder than others, but the difference between starting and not, or playing and not, was very small—you might say 5 percent.

MAKING THE GRADE—AND THEN SOME?

I was extremely lucky to even get into college, as my SATs and GPA in high school were horrible. Anyone who has a teenager looking to go to college or has been to college himself knows that a slight increase in your grade point average has a dramatic effect on your chances of getting into better schools. As I mentioned above, when you go up a level—for instance, from a state school to a small ivy league school—with respect to admittance, if you have a 3.2 GPA versus a 3.6 GPA and all other factors being equal, well, you know the answer. When you go up to the top tier of colleges, even smaller margins will have an impact on your chances. Now, there are a lot of data out there about what colleges look at, and some remain very secretive, but common sense and the research I have done have allowed me to make the simple conclusion—slight increases without a doubt will have an impact on your chances. I wish I realized that earlier than I did.

My first semester in college I earned a 2.75 GPA, and I must say that I was somewhat relieved. I hadn't failed anything, I didn't get any Ds, but I knew it was time to buckle down and improve those grades. I don't remember any of the other semesters except two. My sophomore year, I got a D in a class, which hurt my GPA, and my senior year last semester I think I got a 3.9 GPA. After four years, for many of which I was on the Dean's List, I graduated with a respectable 3.0. Congratulations to me, right? Sure, it was a great accomplishment to graduate college, especially on time. But now what? Now I was one of all of the other college graduates trying to figure out what I was going to do with my life. I wasn't really special; I didn't really have an edge. How was I going to get that slight edge? My plan was to go to law school.

LAW SCHOOL—THEN WHAT?

I now had a pretty simple idea and plan: take my decent but not great grades and squeak my way into a law school, become a lawyer, and then change the world. Well, if I had done just a little bit better, all that would have been a lot easier to accomplish.

Many people believe true success is built through struggle and I don't totally disagree, but if *you* can improve your chances by just trying a little bit harder, then the struggles outside of your control will not seem so daunting.

Being young in college and not really appreciating how competitive the next level of education was like, looking back maybe I would have tried just a little bit harder. In order to get into law school, you need to take the LSAT test, which is essentially the law school version of the SAT. I took a couple of practice exams and even took a six-week course to prepare me for the exam. On my practice tests, I was scoring right in the middle of the pack. I was working pretty much every day selling cars and studying and going to class at night. When I actually took the exam, my results were abysmal. I scored in the lower 30 percentile and I was devastated. I felt like my life was over. I remember being a complete mess and going into a funk. But I decided I wasn't going to give up and I was going to study again and give the exam another shot. I tried a little bit harder, spent more time in the library, and took another six-week course. I was testing about the same in the practice exams, which I was happy with. The second time around, I got the exact same score as the previous exam. Now my life was really over; I was going to be relegated to being a car salesperson my whole life, which is what I was doing while applying to law school. Not that there is anything wrong with that profession, but that is not what I saw for myself. I had bigger plans. I wanted to change the world. I really did! So there I was—I had tried a little bit harder but it didn't make any difference at all! What did that mean?

Despite your efforts, sometimes the immediate result you are looking for and expect won't happen. That doesn't mean you need to give up and throw in the towel. I was determined to go to law school and become a lawyer. My grades in college were decent with a 3.0, my extracurricular activities were solid, and I knew I had to at least try. At this level in academia it really is the small things that separate people from acceptance to rejection. So I decided I was going to go out and try harder than others in my exact situation. I wasn't the only person in the country who had bombed the LSAT and had a B average. I knew that some of those people were going to get into law school and I just needed to outshine those people. So I devised a plan. I would work harder than them on my essays, I would get great recommendations, and I would do just a little bit more than all the others would have done.

Law schools don't have an interview process, at least they didn't when I applied. But I was able to convince the schools to interview me. I reached out to my friends and relatives and asked them if they knew anyone at the schools I wanted to get into. My best friend Kevin's dad, whom I talk about in *Ask More, Get More*, knew a professor at Suffolk University Law School and he agreed to sit down with me. Kevin's dad is a classic hard-working, blue-collar, salt-of-the-earth guy. He is a very successful businessman who owned his own machine shop, but he also made very high-end pool cues. He knew the professor because they both shared a passion for pool and Kevin's dad sold the dean some very expensive pool cues. The dean wasn't on the admissions committee but had been at the school a long time. I went into Boston and met with him. I remember the exhilarating feeling of just being on the campus. The energy was intoxicating, and it solidified my determination more than ever to go to law school. In our meeting, I told him why I wanted to go to law school, and he was very candid with me about how difficult law school really is. In a way, he was trying to talk me out of applying. Looking back, he was in reality just trying to rattle my cage and see how serious I was. He wanted to look me in the eye and see if I was really ready.

In addition to reaching out to the professor, I reached out to the district attorney who had crucified me in high school for being friends with a boy in my neighborhood who had killed his girlfriend. I tell this story in *Ask More, Get More*, but the point here is that I was willing to go the extra mile; it wasn't too time-consuming, it was just being able to do a little bit more to improve my chances to get into law school. Some people would not even consider reaching out to someone who was, essentially, an enemy. But if you really want something, you have to not only do things just a little bit better than your competitors; you have to be a little more creative, you have to think a little bit harder.

Asking the district attorney, who had essentially told the world when I was in high school that I was a bad kid, is more than what most people would do. In this situation, I really had nothing to lose, but I needed to do as much as possible to ensure a win. I needed to outwork just by a little bit the other potential candidates.

Well, the summer of 2003 I got a letter that stated I was wait-listed at Suffolk and another Boston law school. I knew then that I had at least done enough to get on the bubble, but I hadn't yet got it. I also got accepted to Quinnipiac Law School in Connecticut, so I knew I was going somewhere, but I wanted to go to Suffolk. Late in the summer, literally days before I was going to pack up and head to Connecticut, I got a phone call from the same professor who had had the informal meeting with me and he told me they had one spot for me in the evening division. He told me I had to make the decision right then and there because there were other potential candidates right behind me. Well, I accepted Suffolk, the school I really wanted to attend. My grades were not the best and my LSAT scores were horrible, but my drive, my work ethic, and my desire to go to law school were just a little bit better than others.

What is the point of this long-winded story about law school? Well, there are a couple. If I had tried a little bit harder in high school, I would have had more opportunities for colleges. And if I had applied myself just a little bit more in college and maybe graduated with a 3.2 to 3.4 GPA, even with poor LSAT results I would have probably been accepted easier and at more schools, giving me more opportunities.

But the other takeaway here is that, despite my efforts in attempting to get a good score on the LSAT, I didn't come out where I wanted to. But I also didn't throw in the towel and I found other ways to be just a little bit better than others. Had I just been average in my efforts post–LSAT exam, I can say with conviction I would not have been accepted.

One final point here: Some people may say that I was doing way more than just 5 Percent More to get in, and compared to society as a whole, my efforts were most likely more than the average, but in this situation, against all of the other candidates, everyone tries hard to get in. Just like the Olympic athlete who is already at the top of the athletic world as a whole, in order to get the gold you have to be just a little bit better, and in this scenario, thank God and thank 5 Percent More, I was.

CHAPTER 2

5 Percent More about 5 Percent More

As I mentioned above, I sold cars right after I graduated college and before I was accepted into law school. I certainly learned a lot on the car lot. There was a tall, skinny, somewhat awkward yet enthusiastic salesperson named Brian there whom I will never forget. He was one of the most upbeat, happy, and vibrant individuals I had ever met: Always excited, and he loved what he did. He taught me so many things, not only about selling cars but about how to approach life. He was also on top of the sales leaderboard month after month, and he always gave just a little more effort every day.

One day, he sold *five* cars. Even for some of the largest dealerships in the country, five in one day is a lot of cars. It was getting late, just before closing on a hot summer night. Brian had already sold those *five* cars and he saw a customer out on the lot. He jumped from his desk and headed out to greet the customer. But just before he did, I asked him why. I said, "Brian, you have already sold five cars." He told me something amazing. He said, "Mike, every day I tell myself I want to just sell one car, then once I sell that car, I tell myself I want to sell just one more, until it is time to go home." Every day, Brian took himself just a little bit further and achieved above-average results. You see, he was working until closing anyway, so why just put the effort in? Why not do just a little bit more? Oh, I bet you are wondering what happened with that customer. Well, he did not sell to that customer that night, but the next day when Brian showed up for work, the customer from the previous night did as well. Brian's efforts gave him a sale the next day.

About a month later, I was finishing up my third sale for the day. I had tied my all-time best day for sales and was in my glory and just excited to go back and sit down and reflect on how good it felt. I will never forget that day. Brian came up to me with a huge smile and congratulated me. Then he looked at me with his effervescent personality and squeaky voice and said, "Now go sell one more, Mikey." I remember feeling this overwhelming exhaustion take over my body when he said it. I felt like I had already achieved so much for that day. But it was only 2 PM and I was there until 8 PM. He could see that I was tired and wanted to just sit for a while, but he then brought me to where the leaderboard was. This board showed all of us salespeople where we were for the month. I had hit 15 cars that day, and it was close to my all-time high. Now, sales is a very competitive environment, and Brian was just another sales-person, and he certainly did not make money on my sales. In fact, I could possibly take money from him if I were at the top. We got bonuses if we were at the top. Brian was just two cars ahead of me at 17. The top salespeople had already hit 20 cars for the month and we still were trying to get more. Brian said another profound thing to me: he said, "Mikey, brother, don't you want to be at the top? Don't you want to be just a little bit better? Wouldn't you like a little bit more commission?" I thought to myself, "Of course I do." He then said, "Well, the only way to get this is to just try a little bit harder."

We walked back down those stairs into the showroom as I was still processing what he had said to me. He went off and greeted another customer and then it clicked for me—one more sale! Well, that day I didn't make another sale, but I did greet more customers and try to sell them a car. Some of those customers eventually did buy a car, and I did go on to have the best month I had ever had, selling 22 cars and leading the board that month. That was the only time I ever led the board in my three years of selling cars, but after that month I always tried just a little bit harder than before and was always one of the top salespeople.

Striving for and taking action to be just a little bit better every day may not actually yield better results, but if you don't take the action you will never get there, you will never know if you can be better. Every day after the day that Brian showed me the way to get better, I always tried to push myself just a little bit more. I would come in just a little bit earlier, I would stay later. Sometimes I even came in on my day off if I had nothing going on. Some days it would pay off and some days it wouldn't, but at the end of the month it always showed on the board.

Guess who also did a little bit more: the top salespeople, including Brian, the management, and the owners.

Sometimes you don't achieve your goal that day, but that is not the point. The point is striving for it, day in and day out. Striving to be just a little bit better each and every day will pay off. It took me almost two weeks and several customers before I actually sold my first car. My managers kept telling me to stick around more, greet more customers, do more than the other salespeople and eventually it will happen. And it did!! When I first started, I honestly wasn't even thinking of being the best, I just wanted to sell one car; then the next day, one more. But Brian showed me I could do just a little more each day that would yield long-term results. Do just a little bit more and you will get more, have more, and be more. The car sales profession has always been looked down upon. When people talk negatively about a salesperson in general, they say things like, "That guy treated me like a used car salesman." There are bad car salespeople just like there are bad medical salespeople or produce salespeople. But another interesting fact about the above is that the guys and gals who made real money selling cars, year in and year out, were the ones who did try just a little bit harder. In the three years I sold cars, I saw at least 100 salespeople come and go, but there were always the top eight or nine, always there, always making money no matter how many other salespeople flooded the sales floor. You know why? You guessed it, their 5 Percent More efforts each and every day, month, and year allowed them to build a base of customers that came in to buy directly from them, and they continued to build their base. Their commission stayed the same as if it were a new customer, but their repeat customers were so much easier and, ultimately, allowed the salesperson to make more money!

PERSONAL ACCOUNTABILITY FOR YOUR PERFORMANCE

If you are in business, could 5 Percent More on your bottom line change your world? The answer is yes. As a successful entrepreneur, I have been recognized by publications such as the *Boston Business Journal* and *Inc.* magazine for my business accomplishments. I have launched several companies that generate millions of dollars year in and year out. The big secret is that these accomplishments were achieved through no secret methods at all. In fact, when it comes to some of the complicated business things like earnings, profit and loss statements, EBITA, and all the other boring stuff, I leave that up to the accountants. I know that the fundamental, most basic, thing works—which is, do just a little bit more each and every day as an employee and as a business owner, and you will get more. As a business owner, I expect my employees to do better each and every day. I expect them to improve on their personal goals each and every day, which has a profound impact on the business as a whole.

And that doesn't always mean just doing the same thing you have been doing but more of it. Sometimes it means becoming more aware; more in tune; and more willing to learn, to change, and to grow in new ways. Someone once said to me, "Don't confuse activity with accomplishment." Meaning, just because you are busy does not mean you are accomplishing anything. Statistics and raw business data are the foundation of virtually every business. Moving the needle just one percentage point, let alone five, could mean literally billions of dollars to the large multinational corporations of the world. One percentage point could be the difference between a successful business venture and one that fails. A 5-percent swing in the stock market can cause people great distress or make them want to go out and buy a new house. So you have do whatever it takes to get a little more leverage, a little bit more understanding of what will lead to your success. This is still the 5 Percent More strategy, but in a slightly more complex way.

So, I know you are now asking yourself, "How do I do it? As a business owner, manager, or employee, how do I become more efficient and productive? How can I be 5 percent better? How can I do 5 Percent More for my company?"

As a business owner, I have a few things that I do or a few things that I look at to increase efficiency. First of all, if you are the boss or an employee, you need to be accountable for *your* daily activity. You must be honest with yourself and your accomplishments. One of the best ways is to write down your goals for the day and the week, and each day look back at what you did and didn't accomplish.

I briefly discuss this in *Ask More, Get More*, but some sort of written system for your daily activity is crucial. I have met with efficiency experts who I think sometimes take it almost too far by mapping out every second of every day. If you have never made a daily and weekly goal, I find that on a micro level on a daily and weekly basis will certainly help you become more accountable.

As the boss, implementing daily and weekly goal setting for your employees from the top down will make your team or company more efficient. Every day, every week, every month, my company looks at the performance of our salespeople and our customer service professionals.

If you are the boss, looking at the numbers and discussing how to improve them will have zero effect. You can tell your managers you want to see the numbers increase, and set unrealistic goals, but what really needs to be done is showing them the numbers, showing them how you want them to improve on their individual numbers, and holding them accountable.

Recently, we were really underperforming and needed to get our numbers up. We looked at a lot of metrics, like what we call our revenue per call, or RPC. RPC allows us to figure out how much revenue on average a sales agent is generating. Any sales organization, any good one that is, must always check itself and challenge itself in order to survive. A 5 percent increase in our overall RPC is huge. So, when we looked at our performance, we asked ourselves what we could do to increase our productivity. Some sales trainers like to set minimums and stretch goals to give the salespeople targets. The challenge is, many people—even the best of salespeople—have difficulty meeting goals that are set by management; many of the goals have an arbitrary nature to them and are beyond stretch goals.

So what did we do differently? We gave 5 Percent More thought to how to do it a little bit differently. It was really simple: We spent more time and invested a little more thought and inspiration on training the agents. We got them more excited and also pulled a couple of agents out of the call queue for the product I am talking about. When we made these changes, we increased our RPC in one week from $25.00 to $30.00, a 20 percent increase! That is more than significant. But the real key is, all we asked for out of our agents was just a 5 percent increase. We established a realistic and achievable goal that virtually every agent could hit, and they hit a much higher one. By spending a little more time as a company on training, just a few hours a week, and setting the goal at a 5 percent increase individually, almost everyone thrived and gave us a *net* gain of 20 percent!

THE MANY APPLICATIONS OF 5 PERCENT MORE

So if you are a student, what if you scored 5 percent higher on SATs? What if you were 5 percent faster on the playing field? Either way, you can dramatically increase your chances of getting into college or onto the next level of academia or athletics. If you are in sales, what if you made 5 Percent More sales? To every human being out there, what if you spent 5 Percent More time with your family? What if your income increased by 5 Percent More every year? You can increase your productivity in virtually every aspect of your life by just 5 percent, and it will have long-term and life-changing benefits.

I even apply this principle to addiction and show you how just 5 Percent More or less can save or ruin your life. I'm not a doctor and not trained in addiction, but I can certainly speak about this subject. My father was addicted to coke, my stepfather died of AIDS from shooting heroin, my mother is HIV positive, one of my stepbrothers died from an overdose, my stepmother was addicted to prescription medication, another brother did time for distribution, another brother was in rehab for his heroin addiction, my grandparents were hard-core alcoholics, and I most certainly have an addictive personality. I have been fortunate to become aware of my family history and have not gone down the same path. I detail, through my own personal experiences with family members and data, that just a 5 percent swing one way or the other can, literally, save your life.

I am a fitness enthusiast, meaning I work out pretty much every day in one form or another, but just like a majority of the population, have had struggles staying on track with my diet.

My weight for most of my life has been an issue for me as I am a big guy. If I were to say that I have an addiction to something, it would be to food! I show you how just 5 Percent More exercise, or eating 5 percent better, can have a remarkable impact on your body and mind.

I will discuss my own personal struggles, from anxiety attacks to divorce, and how just 20 minutes a day of something as simple as meditation can prolong your life, prevent disease, and increase productivity. What is exciting about what I found is that you don't need a gym; you don't need money; you just need yourself and a desire to get healthier. No crazy fad diets, no difficult protocols; just 5 Percent More effort and understanding of your personal health. It really works!

Give 5 Percent More to Yourself

CHAPTER **3**

Be 5 Percent More Successful

I have a writer on staff and I was meeting with him a while back. We were just casually discussing his job and how it was going. I asked him how he planned his day. It was awesome how he laid it out. He told me his goal was to write 800 to 1,000 words a day. His objective was to create better and better content for our newsletter. He then went on to say that many times he meets his goal each day then shoots for a slightly higher word count. Maybe then he shoots for between 1,200 and 1,400 words. He doesn't dream about it; he sets small achievable goals and meets them day in and day out. That is how he pursues, achieves, and defines success.

So what is success? Most people think that a successful person is wealthy. They have all the material things they want. Or professionals like doctors and lawyers are by definition successful just because they are in those particular professions.

Success is a moving target. It means different things to different people. I have been asked and even attempted to define success. I now define success in a very simple manner: it is what you want it to be. That's it: success is what you want it to be. No one else can define it. So when others talk about achieving "extreme" success, only you can define that. Success happens every moment of every day. When you get up and have a productive day, that is a success!! When you go to the gym, that is a success!

But how can you achieve the type of success that society defines? The materialistic dream world? That is also easy! You can't just take massive action and change all of your habits over-night (some do and it works, but most fail). These guys out there who are telling you that you need to 10X your life, or that they can show you how, are misleading a majority of the human population. But what really does work is, you just ask yourself for 5 Percent More. Each day you do the same thing. There are so many unrealistic programs and books out there that only work for a fraction of the population. Most of these programs want you to completely and swiftly change your habits. These programs don't work; it's just human nature. Success, whatever you define it as, takes time and doesn't "just happen." Get 5 Percent More, get 5 percent better, and your "success" is within your reach.

FREEZE-POP FANTASIES

When I started my business of alcohol-infused freeze pops, to say I was naïve is an understatement. I had an idea and I knew I didn't want to look back on life and say I had only done that and tried to launch the product. I knew one of the keys to a successful product launch was taking action and implementation of the actual idea. Remarkably, I was able to actually bring the product to market. On a shoestring budget and a crazy idea or some would call a dream, I now had a product that I was able to sell. Later on in the book, I discuss why dreams are bad for life and in business. I certainly had ambition, youth, and drive, but what I didn't have were connections or financial resources or a concrete plan. I didn't know people with money who could help fund my business.

I launched that business with hardly any working capital. When you hear the saying, "He didn't have two nickels to rub together," that was me. In fact, one time when we actually made a big sale, the sales guy working for me ran out of gas and had no money or credit cards. But I had a check in hand. I was in another town and my gas tank was also almost on empty. I remember looking at the center console, because all I had was a bag full of change left to my name. I was able to put together ten dollars in change, five for me to get to him and five for him, so we could drive to the bank and cash the check.

I was dreaming how I could someday be rich and have a successful business selling freeze pops infused with alcohol. To this day I still think it was an amazing idea. But what I lacked were clear-cut goals and objectives and a vision of where I wanted to be, and, more important, how I was going to get there. I also had a short-term plan for implementation, but didn't have an implementation plan for sales, or growth, or raising capital. Someone recently said to me that it is easy to spend money developing and marketing a product; the hard part is spending money marketing a product in order to make sales. My dream was me running around nightclubs with beautiful women with this cool product and just being successful. Problem is, you don't become successful just by dreaming about it.

A DREAM WITHOUT A PLAN IS JUST A DREAM

Many times our dreams literally cloud our judgment and we are not making decisions that are based on reality. Just like an idea without a plan is nothing, a dream without a plan is even worse. For instance, I acted like I was already successful and spent money on things such as T-shirts and promotional girls, but looking back I realize that if I had spent just a fraction of what I spent on things to build brand awareness and spent that money on promotions that drove sales I would have accomplished a lot more. I remember driving into Boston one night on the way to a promotional event we planned at one of the nightclubs and listening to one of our radio spots we purchased. It was so cool! But that's all it was. It had zero value in causing people to actually buy the product. I remember also dreaming about the beat-up blue van we had and wrapping it in our logo and filling it up with promotional girls and pulling up to a club and how awesome that would have looked. It would have looked awesome, but it was literally just a dream; it wasn't even an idea, it was just a dream. It certainly wasn't a plan. If I had just spent a little more time on what really mattered—selling product—who knows where I would be today with that product. I know so many young wannabe entrepreneurs who tell me about their dreams with such enthusiasm and passion. They light up and get so excited about what their dream looks like, but when I ask them one basic question—"What is your plan to get there?" they *all* freeze up and get confused and defensive. The hardest part of accomplishing anything is spending a little more time on the tough stuff, which is developing a plan. I am not a huge fan of business plans, but they serve a purpose. One big purpose is for the entrepreneur to flesh out the viability of the business itself. For purposes of an investor, I think they are useless. But for the entrepreneur, it helps him begin to develop a plan. Spend a little more time on working out your plan and less time on dreaming, and you will achieve your goals.

The problem is that this involves actually giving 5 Percent More than you intended to give. That's the next part of achieving success. Sometimes it's not so much about 5 Percent More of the same thing you have been giving, but 5 Percent More of something different, something that you didn't think you needed to give or even *could* give, but you are willing to give it once you realize what it is.

MAKING MONEY DOING NOTHING

Recently, when I was literally going door to door myself selling Emory Vodka, I was with a young salesperson from my distributor. He is a nice guy and I don't know a lot about him personally. But after one of our stops, he presented me with what I would call a cross between a dream and idea for an apparel company. He showed me a hat with the initials MMDN, which stands for Making Money Doing Nothing. Now, I give him credit for actually implementing his idea. He actually created a product, he created a website, and was much farther along than most "dreamers." The challenge with this, like me with Zeus Juice, he is just dreaming about beautiful women wearing his hats or shirts running around nightclubs while he sits back and looks cool. When he showed me the hat, I didn't say anything other than telling him it doesn't work that way. Meaning, you can't make money by doing nothing selling a brand called Making Money Doing Nothing. This was several weeks ago and I've been thinking about this young man for a while and saw myself in him. He took his quasi-dream/idea and took action to actually create a product. But to really grow it, it is going to take *a lot* more effort. How can I say this in a book titled 5 Percent More? Well, he is going to have to take a look at what it takes to sell apparel, which is a very competitive business, look at the top brands, and do just 5 Percent More than them to really grow— and from ground zero, yes, that is *a lot* more effort. But what he can do is implement the 5 Percent More mentality each and every day to work up to the level where he needs to be. I know this works because I do it every day.

Many times I am asked to help young entrepreneurs and even existing businesses solve their challenges or help them accomplish their goals. The first thing I do is listen to what their "idea" is. Then I ask that question, "What is your plan to accomplish your goal?" I had another guy who came to me and said he wanted to start a T-shirt/apparel company. He had never owned a business, never really sold anything other than drugs, and he was a high school dropout. Needless to say, the cards were not and are not in his favor. His qualifications are irrelevant; some of the richest people in the world lack the education one would think was required for success. He told me how he wanted to target people who follow the jam bands, the Jerry Garcia scene, and attend concerts and festivals. He then went on to tell me how he helps all of these bands by promoting them and getting people to their shows. I was confused; was this a promotional company or an apparel company? A couple other things to note: I really liked his logo and the name of his company. It had more than one meaning and I think could have mass appeal.

So I liked the idea of his apparel company, but he lacked vision and was also a dreamer. He, like me in my Zeus Juice days, had a dream of partying it up with fun people and just being successful, but to make matters worse he also did not have a plan. I recently spent several hours working with him on how to develop a plan, but he just can't do it, and the reason he can't do it is, all he really has is a dream until he can put into place an action plan. And it's not just that he doesn't have that plan; he is not willing to develop that plan. He is not willing to go the extra mile—to give 5 Percent More of something that he didn't think he would need to give. You see, he is actually really close to success, but he needs to do just a little bit more, which he thinks he is, but he's just busy and not accomplishing anything. 5 Percent More production, 5 Percent More accountability, and 5 Percent More effort implementing a plan is all he needs.

One of my biggest mistakes during the Zeus Juice days was not listening to the businesspeople I knew and what they told me. One of the biggest things they asked was what I now asked: "What is your plan to make sales?" I was so set on achieving my dreams that I didn't realize that it was impossible to get to the made-up reality of a dream. I needed a concrete plan, and I refused to look at that because deep down inside I knew I didn't have a plan and I didn't want to face the reality of the fact that the alcohol-infused freeze pop, with a small budget even with a concrete plan, was not going to be successful.

In reality, all I had was a quasi-dream/idea without a plan for implementation. That dream caused me a lot of heartache, including having to file for bankruptcy. Spend just a little bit of time to develop a plan so that you can work toward a goal. Too many people get lost in their dreams and get crushed because they didn't spend just a little bit of time on an action plan. Now, your plan may be completely wrong, but it is better than no plan at all. The great news is, you can adjust your plans ever so slightly to get you to you goal.

5 PERCENT DAYS

There were many reasons why that business didn't work, but one thing to this day still haunts me. I was young, had ambition, and was a hustler. I persevered through some of the most difficult days, like, literally, running on empty and barely making it to the gas station. Like any entrepreneur, I worked my ass off, day in and day out. But there were days when it became too much and I, literally, curled up in a ball and just lay in bed. What haunts me about those days is that those days—and there were only a couple—were the 5 percent days. Those were the lost days that I didn't get up and push through. 5 Percent More shows you how that little extra effort is what really sets people apart in this world. Those 5 percent days that I lost were in the middle of the summer and were days when I could have sold just a little bit more, opened one more account, and met one more client. I still have days when I want to lay in bed and feel bad for myself, and I still succumb to them. But, the difference is, I have done just a little bit more than most for so many consecutive years that my lost days do not have as much of a detrimental effect on my business. I am also now more aware of these types of days and I am able to recognize them and get up and get it done. There is always someone looking to take your spot, and, in order to succeed, you have to just be a little bit better than the rest.

PLAN TO GIVE 5 PERCENT MORE

So, ultimately, success is about 5 Percent More, but it may be giving that 5 percent in ways that you originally weren't prepared to give, or that you thought wasn't necessary. But that's one of the key aspects of 5 Percent More that's so simple and so important. It's about always trying, thinking, giving, and being willing to give a little bit more of all of you. If you are willing to do that in every way, then you are ready to make 5 Percent More out of your life.

CHAPTER **4**

Make 5 Percent More Money

I have been very fortunate to have been able to sponsor a car in the Sprint Cup Series of NASCAR. As a result of my sponsorship I have become close to the owner, Archie St. Hilaire, of Go FAS Racing, a small team based in Maine. I wasn't a NASCAR fan until my company began sponsoring cars with Archie and his team. I was, however, always fascinated with the marketing involved with NASCAR. NASCAR fans are the most loyal fans you will ever meet. NASCAR fans buy clothing with sponsors' names and logos all over them and wear them with pride. Not only are the cars 200-mile-an-hour billboards, but the spectators also become walking advertisements. I have had many conversations with Archie and some of his drivers about what it takes to win a NASCAR event. When I first sponsored a car in the Daytona 500, I wanted us to win. Boy, was I naïve! Then several other sponsorships later, I still wanted to win, but Go FAS is a small team with a small budget. One day at an event we were holding at a local restaurant for the number 32 car, I was talking with the driver, Eddie MacDonald, about winning. Eddie MacDonald has had a lot of success in a lower series but was also driving a car I sponsored in the Sprint Cup, essentially the Major League of racing. I was discussing 5 Percent More and how the speeds of the cars are very close to each other, how the weight of the cars has to be the same, and how the field was, in my view, pretty level. Eddie corrected me about the field not being so level and reminded me of some of the bigger teams and the amount of money they spend to win. Smaller teams like Go FAS have about ten employees, while Joe Gibbs Racing has hundreds of employees with annual budgets north of $100 million a year, all to be a fraction of a percent faster than their competitors. There are several teams with budgets that exceed $100 million annual budgets. Millions of dollars all in order to be just be a little bit faster than everyone else.

In the Sprint Cup, there are 43 cars that race each week. Eddie MacDonald told me that, realistically, a team like Go FAS is racing against twelve teams and they try to get just a little bit better each week. As I type, it still boggles my mind. The likelihood of a small team winning is so unfathomable that pigs would have to fly if a team that small were to win. I went to lunch one day with Archie and Eddie and I asked, "Why do it if you can't win?" Well, they both told me that they of course want to win, but there is a lot more to NASCAR than just winning the overall race. There are points and placements and sponsorships that, if done properly, can be a profitable business, and each year a small team like Go FAS tries to get better, just a little bit each week and each year. This year, as a result of Go FAS getting just a little bit better each and every week, they landed a major multinational sponsor, which will allow them to spend more and, you guessed it, get more, and ultimately get better. The point here is to highlight how far people are willing to go to get that slight edge. That slight edge in NASCAR means the difference between thousands of dollars and millions, hundreds of millions of dollars.

You don't have to spend millions or take huge risks to get the same return on investment; small incremental victories will pay off for you long term, just like it is paying off for Go FAS. Just like every team has to start somewhere and make strides to get just a little bit better, you do, too, and the payoff can be huge.

> Small opportunities are often the beginning of great enterprises.
>
> —DEMOSTHENES

So many people in this day and age expect to just rise to the top. They feel as though they should be the boss or making more money. It doesn't happen that way. The best way to increase your chances of making more money is to do more than what is asked of you—essentially to do 5 Percent More, especially the small things, without the expectation of additional compensation. I have seen this time and time again. Having the opportunity to be a boss and now an owner of a company that has employed hundreds of people, I've seen that the ones who rise to the top, the ones who make more money than everyone else, are the ones who do more than their peers without expectation of additional compensation. By doing a little more than what is expected of you, you are making your company more money, and then, ultimately, you will be pocketing more money yourself.

We will talk about the concept of giving 5 Percent More to others later in the book and how it can lead you to reap so much more riches in general. But for now, let's discuss the concept of how giving 5 Percent More can lead you to make more money in the simplest of ways.

5 PERCENT MENTALITY

While in law school I took a job in a call center in a basement of a building with no windows. I had just declared bankruptcy, was about to get married, stressed about keeping my grades up, and needed money badly. Having no money and trying to finish law school while moving forward with my life, I must say, was very difficult. It was very humbling and I had to rely on a lot of people, including my girlfriend and soon-to-be wife at the time.

Working in a call center in a dark basement of a turn-of-the-century old building that used to manufacture shoes seemed like a step back in life. I had started a business—the juice pops—that I believed was going to be huge, but ultimately didn't work, and I was in law school but now working in a call center with people who, quite frankly, were not the most respected members of society. Many of them had dependency issues, some were in and out of jail, others were actually on the ankle bracelet. Yet here I was, a soon-to-be law school graduate in the same call center as drug addicts and people on a work-release program. It was not very good for my ego. However, it was a great opportunity to make money and be successful, and that's exactly what I did.

Initially, I was just a call center agent who made sales and got paid a commission. As someone who had sales experience and training, plus my motivation to make money, I rose to the top very fast. I wasn't always the best as there were a few guys and gals there who had better sales skills than me, but I was in the top 5 or 10 percent every week. I worked week in and week out a legitimate seventy hours a week. We had to actually punch in and out every week, and I remember seeing 70 to 72 hours every week on the punch card. But that effort paid off as well. I was pacing about $75,000 a year working in a call center that also gave me the flexibility to finish law school and then study for the bar exam.

The company announced an opportunity to interview for and become a team leader on the sales floor. As a team leader, I would be responsible for roughly a dozen or so other sales agents and I would be compensated by receiving a small override on my team commission. The catch was, if I wasn't on the phones making my own sales I wouldn't be making money for myself. There were roughly 10 other team leaders on the sales floor. Many of them were very nervous about losing their own commissions while having to improve their teams. I thought differently from all of them. I looked at this opportunity as a way to increase my personal *net worth* and my *net worth* to the company. Meaning, if I was able to show that I could improve my team's numbers week in and week out, I would not only receive my override but I would also become an asset to the company. But what it took was a mentality that said I wasn't going to give just 5 Percent More of my time or my effort. I was already doing that. But I had to agree to give 5 Percent More of something different, something that I wasn't necessarily ready to give. I had to be open to giving 5 Percent More in a way that at first seemed contrary to what I wanted to achieve. I had to be open to opening my mind 5 Percent More. And it led to me making a *whole* lot more money.

Each week, I spent just a small amount of time with my team. I used the limited tools we had, from spreadsheets to e-mail, to help keep my team motivated and accountable. We had brief meetings and goal-setting sessions each week and we went over the previous week's numbers. I sent daily motivating quotes and updated the team periodically on where they were at hitting their goals. Here is the interesting thing. My personal commissions were never affected and my team was consistently the top team generating more revenue for the company week in and week out. I just spent a little bit of time, but quality time, with my team that made me *more* money as a whole and increased my net worth to the company.

All of the other team leaders resented me and thought I was somehow gaming the system and cheating. Some of the smarter ones would come to me and *ask* what I was doing and I would show them how a simple system that took relatively little time paid out significant dividends. I spent maybe an hour a week, roughly 1 percent of the working hours each week—not 5 percent, just 1 percent—and it changed my life.

Rather than worrying about how this was going to be just a responsibility or a burden that was going to be negative, like most of my colleagues, I took this opportunity; spent a little bit of time and increased my *net worth* significantly. This small amount of time that I spent is what, ultimately, led me to making millions of dollars.

According to the U.S. Census Bureau, a family of four in 2014 with a yearly income at or under $24,091 is considered to be at the poverty level.[1] According to the United States Department of Agriculture in that same year, the cost to feed that family ranges from $150 to $298 per week.[2] Without adjusting for taxes, the food alone is roughly half of a family's weekly check. How can anyone live this way? Well, I lived that way when I was a kid. So, what people are left to do is improvise and adapt, and many times the improvisation is cheaper, less nutritious food, or resort to crime. I did both as a kid. Now, I haven't even discussed rent, food, travel expenses, and other basic necessities. What if that same family found a way to make just 5 Percent More income? That would be another $1,200 a year. What would that do for them? Well, for starters it would give them the ability to save that money. What if they found a way to make 5 Percent More each year? How would that impact their lives? What if they allotted 5 Percent More of their time to finding ways to make money? Well, I've seen how it works firsthand. The most my mother made at her full time job was about $19,000 a year, raising me and my brother. We were at the poverty level. What did she do to help get more for us? On the weekends, early morning, she delivered newspapers. She dragged me and my little brother out of bed at 5 AM on Saturday every week so she could make another hundred a week. This was a small effort. Was it hard? Sure. Did it hurt her ego? Sure it did. But that small effort for a few hours a week increased her total income by close to 30 percent. Look, we were poor, not the poorest of poor, but I never felt like I was going without because of the small efforts that my mom made. When I look at some of the other kids living at the poverty level like me, we had a much better life. All because of a little more effort my mom put in. So, if this is you, if you are at that level, you can find a way to make more money. It doesn't matter what the job is or, really, how much money you make. Make just a little bit more and grow it. It will take time, but you will get out of it. You really will! As I type these words it is difficult to articulate my emotional state because I was at or below the poverty level for just under half of my life and now I'm a millionaire. I've seen it, lived it, and know it can be done.

There are research and data out there that discuss why the majority of poor people will remain poor. But when you dig through all the research and data, one thing the data don't provide is any substantive solution. The real answer is that poor people lack the skills to break through. Not skills as in a trade, but the knowledge and know-how to pull themselves out. Not even the drive. Just the "where do I start" part or "how do I start." How do I know this? Well, the scientific community agrees, but no one really provides the answers. You see, growing up poor, when we got a "windfall"—which was usually our tax returns—my mom and the other people in our neighborhood didn't save this money. We went out and bought new furniture or a bigger television or some other material item to make us feel better. But what was really happening is that we were just digging a deeper hole and becoming more "comfortable" being poor. It is extremely difficult if you are who I am describing right now to believe that little baby steps, micro-successes, are the answer to poverty, but it is really that simple. It is such a huge problem that no one really knows how to address. I am not suggesting that if you do something 5 Percent More every day you are going to eradicate poverty, but what I am saying is that by doing 5 Percent More each and every day you will eradicate *your* poverty. When you get going, give them a copy of this book. Then we can start to make real change.

This will blow your mind if you haven't already seen this: Did you know that saving a penny a day and doubling it each day for 30 days, you will end up with more than $5 million? I said this to my assistant and she responded, "You'd better check your math." So I did and it's below:

Day 1	$.01	Day 16	$327.68
Day 2	$.02	Day 17	$655.36
Day 3	$.04	Day 18	$1,310.72
Day 4	$.08	Day 19	$2,621.44
Day 5	$.16	Day 20	$5,242.88
Day 6	$.32	Day 21	$10,485.76
Day 7	$.64	Day 22	$20,971.52
Day 8	$1.28	Day 23	$41,943.04
Day 9	$2.56	Day 24	$83,886.08
Day 10	$5.12	Day 25	$167,772.16
Day 11	$10.24	Day 26	$335,544.32
Day 12	$20.48	Day 27	$671,088.64
Day 13	$40.96	Day 28	$1,342,177.28
Day 14	$81.92	Day 29	$2,684,354.56
Day 15	$163.84	Day 30	$5,368,709.12

Now, even though this is so simple, the average person, especially those at or below the poverty level, will not be able to get past the second week. Why? Well, you are doubling the amount every day, increasing by 100 percent. Now if you did the same with a penny and increased by 5 percent every day and compounded each and every day for 30 days, or even 60 days, you wouldn't have much. But what if you upped the stakes and started with $100.00? What if you increased that amount by just 5 percent every day, then what would you have? Well, below is the answer:

Day 1	$100.00	Day 3	$110.25
Day 2	$105.00	Day 4	$115.76

Day 5	$121.55	Day 33	$476.49
Day 6	$127.63	Day 34	$500.32
Day 7	$134.01	Day 35	$525.33
Day 8	$140.71	Day 36	$551.60
Day 9	$147.75	Day 37	$579.18
Day 10	$155.13	Day 38	$608.14
Day 11	$162.89	Day 39	$638.55
Day 12	$171.03	Day 40	$670.48
Day 13	$179.59	Day 41	$704.00
Day 14	$188.56	Day 42	$739.20
Day 15	$197.99	Day 43	$776.16
Day 16	$207.89	Day 44	$814.97
Day 17	$218.29	Day 45	$855.72
Day 18	$229.20	Day 46	$898.50
Day 19	$240.66	Day 47	$943.43
Day 20	$252.70	Day 48	$990.60
Day 21	$265.33	Day 49	$1,040.13
Day 22	$278.60	Day 50	$1,092.13
Day 23	$292.53	Day 51	$1,146.74
Day 24	$307.15	Day 52	$1,204.08
Day 25	$322.51	Day 53	$1,264.28
Day 26	$338.64	Day 54	$1,327.49
Day 27	$355.57	Day 55	$1,393.87
Day 28	$373.35	Day 56	$1,463.56
Day 29	$392.01	Day 57	$1,536.74
Day 30	$411.61	Day 58	$1,613.58
Day 31	$432.19	Day 59	$1,694.26
Day 32	$453.80	Day 60	$1,778.97

You would certainly have a lot more than 5 Percent More; 60 days later, you will actually have 1,678 percent more than what you started with. Think you could figure out a way to just save 5 Percent More of the amount of the previous day, every day? If you tried, I bet almost everyone could.

What about your retirement? What will 5 percent do for you long term? I asked my Human Resources manager to project what it would look like if a person who is making $40,000 a year contributed just 5 percent of their weekly pay into a 401(k), and this is what it looks like:

According to Paychex calculators (our payroll company), assuming an 8 percent return, a person (single with 0 allowances) who has 5 percent deducted from their pay for 401(k) with no employer contribution:

Weekly Gross Pay $769.23
Federal Withholding $94.11
Social Security $47.69
Medicare $11.15
Massachusetts $34.60
401(k) Plan $38.46
Net Pay $543.22

Over the 10 years, you would invest $20,000. At 8 percent growth, you would end up with $30,108.57 at the end of 10 years. All this assumes that laws don't change and that the person doesn't receive raises. However, usually over 10 years a person would see some salary increase, and if the contribution stayed at 5 percent, you would save more and have more. Now, it is debatable as to what the stock market has returned over the years, but it is more than 8 percent and some even argue it's more like 12 percent. If you could contribute just $38 a week, you will have, conservatively, $30,000 in 10 years. That $30,000, if left untouched and if you continued to add, would grow and would enable you to have a better life in the future. Just 5 percent. I know the economy still isn't perfect and I know what it is like to struggle, because most of my life I have struggled financially, and I have watched my family members struggle and continue to work without a penny saved. Not one penny! If you are 20, 30, 40, 50 years of age, it doesn't matter, ask yourself what your life will look like in 10 years and then think about not having any savings, and stop and think how that feels deep down inside. Then think about how you would feel if you had some money saved, and how that feels. I know how it feels because in my twenties and early thirties I had zero and it didn't feel good. Even though I own my company and we also do a match, I contribute every week and encourage all of my employees who qualify to contribute. Just 5 percent into your 401(k) will not only make you feel better and relieve stress in the future, but it will enable you to do some of the things you want to in the future.

Ultimately, using the 5 Percent More concept to make more money starts with giving a little bit more effort, a little more dedication, and a little bit more sweat. But finally, it's about changing your mind. Making more money is a mind-set of more. And it begins with believing that just a little bit more money can become a lot more down the road, instead of just trying to get rich quick.

That's how the wealthiest people in the world think. And once you start thinking like that you will be on your way. Growing up poor, I did not think like this. Most poor people do not think like this. Most of us dream about the day when we retire, but we aren't even properly preparing for it. Take a look around you and see if others are properly preparing.

When my daughter was born, my then-wife and I wanted to do the responsible thing and start a college fund. We had a financial services company come to the house. They put together this giant three-ring binder and presentation that said in no uncertain terms no matter how much I made, we were never going to be able to save enough. They basically told us we had already lost. They were creating fear in us like I have never seen before. Almost as bad was the home security guy who ingrained the image of my infant daughter being snatched from her room in the middle of the night if I didn't buy his system. The financial services approach must work, but it made me want to just say, "Fuck it, I will deal with it later." Well, I am halfway there to later (my daughter is 10). That day, we started contributing a modest amount of money into a 529 plan and a savings account for my daughter. Is it going to be enough? Absolutely not; they were right. But it is something, it will most likely be more than half of what she will need, and it is tax deductible.

The point of this is that you have to start somewhere. There is value in momentum and consistency. The modest amount we put in every month has gradually gone up as my income has gone up, and it is just a part of our expenses. Don't think small things can't have a huge impact, because they can.

CHAPTER 5

Be 5 Percent Smarter

Every year, my company gives out several scholarships to deserving students from the high school I graduated from. I do this for several reasons, but one big reason is that giving back to your community is just as important as the hard work someone puts in to become successful. In other words, giving back is a very critical key to long-term success.

Every year, I am utterly amazed at the applications we get. Many of these students have higher than a 4.0 GPA, which I didn't even realize was possible, because of taking AP classes that reward you with an extra point on the scale for the effort. It all made ruling out applicants a very difficult task. But what makes it easier is the students who just filled out a quick form and sent it in without spending the time to fill out the application properly. I immediately eliminate them from potential recipients of the scholarship.

Then when I look at the actual remaining contenders it becomes very difficult to choose. All of these students are at the top of their class, all of them participate in extracurricular activities, and many of them also play a varsity sport. But what I look for is the little extra effort in their application, and that usually is in the form of an essay or letter. When the students write a letter explaining why they deserve the scholarship or explaining a possible anomaly in their transcript, it really helps me decide. We usually give only two scholarships each year, but last year several students stood out. They all spent a little extra time on their application and it paid off.

You see, all of these students are "book smart," but in this instance they were just a little bit smarter than their peers with our scholarship, and this could mean the difference between a private, highly acclaimed academic institution or a decent state school, which ultimately can change the trajectory of someone's life. Smarter doesn't always mean what your transcript reads, but thinking about how to get to the next level and taking action is equally, if not more, important.

Again, here we see the idea of 5 Percent More meaning so much more than just simple extra effort. It means thinking differently.

TEAM LEADER TO GENERAL COUNSEL

As I mentioned in my book *Ask More, Get More*, I missed passing the bar exam by one question. *One question!* That small percentage of the overall exam was the difference between passing and failing. I often wonder what my life would be like if I had spent just a little more time studying and preparing, and if I had passed. To be clear, I don't think about missing the bar exam the first time around negatively and thinking my life may have been better or worse; rather, I think about what my trajectory would have looked like. Would I have been able to achieve the success I have now in the amount of time I have or would it have taken me longer? It was and never is a matter of "if"; it is/was a matter of "when." The bar exam is not something that you can haphazardly study for and expect to pass. You are competing against law school graduates all across the country and they are all working hard to pass. I didn't pass for one reason, and that was lack of effort. I missed by one question because I didn't study enough. When you get to the next level in education everyone works hard, but in order to get to your next peak in your career, you need to do just a little bit more than you did last time. Every hill you climb, you have to work just a little bit harder to get to the next peak.

After missing the bar exam, I studied for thirteen weeks straight and only worked a few days. I studied for thirteen weeks because that is what it takes to pass the bar exam. I wasn't going to leave it up to chance or be willing to risk not passing. Every other serious candidate was doing the same thing, and I was going to do more than all of them. I went to law school to be a lawyer, and passing the bar exam is the final exam. Passing that exam or not passing that exam is life-changing. Ultimately, I did pass the bar exam. I remember where I was when I found out that I had passed—I was in the call center when my wife at the time called me and told me that I had mail from the Board of Bar Overseers. The second time around taking the bar exam was in February, and you don't find out your results until November. When she called, we discussed whether or not she should open it, or whether I should come home. The suspense was too great and I asked her to open it. Well, thankfully, I had passed. It is one of those moments in life that a person always remembers. I can actually see myself in the dark call center with only a few other agents there and screaming that I had passed!!

Passing was just the beginning. Now I needed a job! The good news was that the company I was working for needed an in-house lawyer. Now, this was a fairly large company doing millions in revenue. I had no idea about how the business actually operated, nor did I understand or fully appreciate the legalities of such a large business. I had zero legal experience other than an internship in the district attorney's office. I had a decent academic career where I graduated in the top half of my class and spent three years on the dean's list. But I'm from Boston, where we have the best colleges in the world. I graduated from Suffolk Law, a well respected but low-tier blue-collar working man's law school. I did receive a top-notch education, and some of the best lawyers in the country went to

Suffolk Law, but once you are competing for a job in the legal profession the competition is beyond fierce.

After I passed the bar exam, I immediately began to formulate my plan for getting hired at the company I was working at. I knew I wouldn't be able to compete with lawyers who actually had legal experience, especially from schools like Harvard or Boston College. But what I did have was a basic understanding of the company and my track record. Working in the call center and generating millions in revenue from my team certainly got the attention of the owners. But I had an uphill battle, as the wife of one of the owners didn't like me. She was a legal secretary and thought she could handle all of the legal work. She had major inferiority issues and did not like the idea of having someone like me in a high-level position helping to improve the company. It is such a foolish way to think, and many do think like her. She tried her best to sabotage my hiring, even providing the owners with information stating that I was only worth about $40,000 a year. So I really had to impress the owners! I actually interviewed five times!

During my first interview, I presented the owners with more than just a resume, I showed them how my team had been the best. I showed them how I was one of the top agents as well. I showed them that my *net worth* to them was more than just as a lawyer. Finally, after overcoming some political obstacles related to the owner's wife not liking me, I was hired. What really set me apart from other potential candidates was that less-than-5-Percent-More effort as a team leader that showed the owners how good I really was.

WHAT IF YOUR SAT SCORE WAS HIGHER?

All that being said about my less-than-stellar test results earlier, what if you did finish 5 percent higher in your high school class, what would your life have looked like, or what does it look like if you are still in high school?

Let me give you a quick example of what a slight increase in the GPA and SAT could do for a high school student. The University of Oregon's Presidential Scholarship requires both a 1240 SAT (verbal and math) and a 3.85 GPA.[1]

Suppose you have a student with a pre-SAT score of 1200 and a GPA sitting at 3.7. If this student increases both these figures by 5 percent, he/she would have an SAT score of 1260 and a GPA of 3.89—enough to qualify for the scholarship. The challenge is that even a 5 percent increase needs to be done over time; attempting to get there the last semester of a high school student's senior year would be extremely difficult. As a parent, encourage your children to get a little bit better each exam, each week, and each semester. That slight increase could save a parent hundreds of thousands of dollars in tuition and mean the difference between an Ivy League school or acceptance into a prestigious program and a foundation that sets up a young adult for future success.

So, in a sort of roundabout way, this student could greatly improve his long-term quality of life by increasing his GPA/SAT scores by 5 percent. Below are a couple of examples of GPA/SAT-dependent scholarships.

Scholarship Links
- https://financialaid.uoregon.edu/scholarships_freshmen
- https://scholarships.tamu.edu/FRESHMEN/Available-Scholarships#0-AcademicScholarships
- http://uh.edu/financial/undergraduate/types-aid/scholarships/#academic-excellence-scholarship
- https://mansfield.osu.edu/future-students/admissions/scholarships.html
- http://www.umass.edu/umccc/financial-matters
- http://www.uky.edu/financialaid/scholarship-incoming-freshmen

HIGH SCHOOL GRAD/COLLEGE GRAD INCOME GAP

For long-term success, a reasonable person would agree that a college degree is better than no college degree. There are plenty of examples of people who have been wildly successful without a college degree, but on a larger scale those examples, like Bill Gates, are really few and far between. Parents always wish for and dream about their kids going to and graduating college. But why? Well, data have shown that many college students are underemployed and thus the loans that they accumulated and time they spent may be looked at as a waste. That may very well be true, and the reason is that there are so many kids whose parents dream about them going to college, who figure out a way to get them into a college even though their grades were subpar, and then when they get to college they continue to just be average. An article in *US News* in 2014, however, showed that despite the underemployment of college students the gap between college graduates and nongraduates is growing.[2] In 1965, the gap in yearly earnings was just about $7,500. Today, it is $17,500 on an annual basis. The article explains that college graduates may not be "doing better" than nongraduates, but that the income earning potential for non–college graduates is actually decreasing while college graduates' earnings are increasing. So why do you want to go to college? Why do you want your kids to go to college? It's not about the money, it's about quality of life. Is college the answer to society's problems? Absolutely not. But a 5 percent increase in a high schooler's grades and test scores can give him or her the opportunity to have a better life.

LSAT/GRE

So you graduated college; now what? I remember that feeling. The feeling of accomplishment and pride when I graduated, then followed up with fear and anxiety about what is next. Throughout *5% More*, we talk about doing just a little bit better at each level. Once you graduate college, the next level is, of course, graduate school or medical school or law school. Now, for the LSAT, which is for law school, it is very competitive. For example, let's say that a student gets an LSAT score of 164. If he takes the test again and improves his score by slightly less than 5 percent, his score would rise to 172. That's a huge leap in terms of LSAT scores; for UCLA (just to give an example), the 25th percentile score is 162 (roughly the percentile I was in when I took the test), while the 75th percentile is 169.[3]

Law schools are now required to report only a student's highest score. So instead of averaging the scores of multiple LSAT attempts, like it was when I went to law school, most law schools will now accept just your highest score. So, when I scored the exact same score twice, it actually lowered me a point. That isn't the case now. Good news: if you have a bad day or two or three, you can keep taking the exam. The links for this topic are below.

For the GRE test, a small scoring increase can make a huge difference in percentile. A score of 155 on the Verbal Subtest is in the 67th percentile; by increasing this score slightly more than 5 percent, you would have a score of 163, which is in the 92nd percentile.[4] This is huge! Small increases in these exams and in one's grades can have a lifetime of benefits.

Importance of LSAT

- www.usnews.com/education/blogs/law-admissions-lowdown/2012/ 11/12/learn-the-5-deciding-factors-in-law-school-admissions

LSAT Scores for Top 25 Law Schools

- http://testprep.about.com/od/thelsat/f/GoodLSAT.htm

How Law Schools Evaluate LSAT Scores

- www.usnews.com/education/blogs/law-admissions-lowdown/ 2014/07/21/understand-how-law-schools-evaluate-lsat-scores
- http://testprep.about.com/od/thelsat/f/Multiple_LSATScores_ FAQ.htm

HOW DO WE ENSURE A SUCCESSFUL CHILD?

There is a great book by Paul Tough called *How Children Succeed*, which tries to find out what makes our youth successful. Is it their SAT or ACT scores? Do their surroundings really matter? Can IQ determine future success? Without giving away the book, there are many factors involved, but what is clear is that small gains and small advantages can certainly *help* a child along. Character traits such as integrity, grit, discipline, empathy, and others are also intangible traits that are in many instances more important than what a child's IQ is or how well he does on a standardized test.

That doesn't mean you shouldn't and don't need to worry about doing 5 Percent More on those tests. As discussed throughout this chapter, the amazing benefits of doing better on those tests speak for themselves. But in the long run, being smarter isn't just about these scores; it's about learning how to live smarter. And that means thinking 5 Percent More than the next guy about how to succeed, how to live, how to accomplish your goals.

If you can accomplish that, then you will reap a whole lot more than 5 Percent More.

CHAPTER **6**

Be 5 Percent
Stronger and Faster

When I played football in college I immediately noticed that every player on the team experienced some success in high school, whether it be all state, record breaking at their school, or just leading their league in some statistic. What I also realized is that for the most part we were on a pretty level playing field. I joke around and say we were all high school heroes but now we are starting as college zeros.

By the time I was a junior, the sophomore class was pretty well stocked with talent. There were a couple of guys who got a lot of playing time and a few who seemed to stand out. One guy who played center on offense was a standout in more ways than one. He was an incredible physical specimen at 19. Now, he wasn't the biggest guy on the team and wasn't that big at all, but he was all muscle, and it was rumored that he held the title of Mr. Teen USA. He always seemed to work just a little bit harder than others. When we were finished with our required weight training, he would stay longer. He wasn't the most gifted athletically, but he was always working harder than his peers in his class and the rest of the team. This guy also just stood out in other ways. He seemed to take things slightly more seriously than everyone else; he cared more about football.

He eventually started at center. Now, we were a Division III team, so we weren't that big, but for a center he was barely 210, which is usually the weight of a running back or safety. But because he took the sport more seriously, he studied film more than the rest of the team, and he spent more time in the weight room, he went on to be an NCAA Division II All-American and inducted into the Hall of Fame at Springfield College. One other interesting thing about this guy is, he is now one of the biggest WWE superstars of all time: John Cena.

If you look at Cena's career early on, it was not immediate success, but he just hung in there and worked a little bit harder. Eventually, that hard work dating back to his days in high school and Springfield College paid off and has made him the mega-star he is today. He worked just a little bit harder in college, then worked harder early on in the WWE, and he achieved success that I'm sure even he didn't realize was possible.

ELITE ATHLETES AND WHAT 5 PERCENT MEANS

I want to present you with some pretty compelling data as it relates to elite athletes and their counterparts. First, let's take a look at Tiger Woods, arguably one of the best professional golfers of all time.

Below is a list of matches he won and the difference between him and tenth place.

		Tiger	**Tenth**	
1997	Masters	270	286	5.59%
2001	Masters	272	280	2.86%
2002	Masters	276	285	3.16%

		Tiger	**Tenth**	
2005	Masters	276	285	3.16%
2000	US Open	272	291	6.53%
2002	US Open	277	286	3.15%
2008	US Open	283	288	1.74%
2000	Open Championships	269	280	3.93%
2005	Open Championships	274	281	2.49%
2006	Open Championships	270	279	3.23%
1999	PGA Championship	277	285	2.81%
2000	PGA Championship	270	279	3.23%
2006	PGA Championship	270	279	3.23%
2007	PGA Championship	272	281	3.20%

The difference between winning and tenth place in these major championships is so incredibly small. One or two strokes could mean the difference in hundreds of thousands of dollars.

Now let's take a look at the most decorated Olympian of all time, Michael Phelps. He has had some personal struggles of late, but that doesn't diminish what he has accomplished in the pool.

		First	**Last**	**Difference**	**Change**
PHELPS					
2012	100 Butterfly	00:51.21	00:52.05	00:00.84	1.6%
2008	200 Individual Medley	01:54.20	02:00.80	00:06.50	5.4%
2008	200 Butterfly	01:52.00	01:55.10	00:03.10	2.7%
2008	200 Freestyle	01:43.00	01:47.50	00:04.50	4.2%
2008	400 Individual Medley	04:03.80	04:15.40	00:11.60	4.5%
2004	100 Butterfly	00:51.25	00:52.56	00:01.31	2.5%
2004	200 Butterfly	01:54.00	01:57.50	00:03.40	2.9%

Or what about Usain Bolt, one of the fastest men on the planet?

		First	Last	Difference	Change
BOLT					
2012	100	9.63	11.99	2.36	19.7%
2012	200	19.32	20.69	1.37	6.6%
2008	100	9.69	10.03	0.34	3.4%
2008	200	19.30	20.59	1.29	6.3%

In all but one, the percentage between first and last were very close.

So, are these athletes just gifted? Were they blessed by the Almighty with their talents? Some would say yes, but when you look at what it really takes, they were just a little bit better than the rest in their field.

I was recently in Miami and I saw a man standing on Lincoln Road selling a book. I saw him on three separate occasions standing hawking his book. As an entrepreneur, I loved it, so I decided to speak to him. His name is Maubrey Destined and he is a native of Nigeria. His book was a story about his life. I read some of it, but his book or selling it wasn't the interesting thing. He was selling his book to support his training for the 2016 Olympics. We discussed what his training entailed, but more important, I asked him what his time was. He claimed was running just over a 10.07 in the 100 meters, which would not get him a medal. All he is striving for is a time that is just 5 percent better, which would potentially get him the gold and the world record. It was surreal when he said it to me, that that is all it takes to go from a fast guy to an Olympian. In the 1992 Olympics, Frank Fredericks got the silver with a 10.02 time, but since then every medalist in the 100 meter except for Obasele Thompson in Sydney in 2000 got on the podium with a time under

10.00. If Maubrey Destined does in fact get 5 percent better, his time would be a 9.56 and would set the world record. As I type today, the current world record holder is Usain Bolt with a 9.58 time in 2009.

Now, this may seem impossible to some, but again we are only looking for a 5 percent better time than what he is getting right now. But if you look at Usain Bolt and his times historically, the difference between one of his worst times in 2007 with a 10.03 and his best time in 2009 with 9.58 was just under 5 percent, and the wind differential was essentially the same, with a +0.7 and +0.9 respectively.[1]

But if Usain Bolt, one of the most gifted athletes of our time, was asked to get 50 percent better or change his times by even 10 percent, for all intents and purposes it would be impossible. I bring this up and look at someone like Usain Bolt to highlight how an elite athlete like Usain Bolt is looking to get just 5 percent better, which is what puts him into the category of greatness.

You, too, can change things by just 5 percent and achieve greatness. But forget greatness, just get better. I will admit that it may be hard to compare the average, everyday person to someone like Usain Bolt, but stop for a second and think about what it takes for Usain Bolt to actually achieve a 5 percent differential to get the gold and what you need to do to change or get 5 Percent More, which would, arguably, be much less difficult since you are probably not operating at near capacity right now.

Elite athletes like Usain Bolt train practically every day and their "job" is really the sport in which they participate. But so does every world-class athlete. So what is the point? The point is, Usain Bolt in many races, not just the majors is barely 5 percent better than his counterparts and he is the world record holder and a multi-gold Olympian. In your field, in the field of life, if you are just 5 percent better or try 5 percent harder, or come close, you will achieve greatness.

GROW, BABY, GROW

> The last three or four reps is what makes muscle grow.
> This area of pain divides the champion from someone
> else who is not a champion.
>
> —Arnold Schwarzenegger

When we work out in the gym, most of us are there to maintain our health and for vanity. In other words, we want to look good. I have been going to the gym pretty regularly my entire life. As a result of that, I have tried many programs and routines in an effort to achieve greater results. I have trained specifically for football, I have trained specifically to lose fat, I have trained for speed, and just for strength. Right now, I'm training for strength. Some people wonder why a 40-year-old who isn't playing competitive sports would want to do that. Well, the answer is simple for me. It just works for me. I feel better, I sleep better, and I accomplish more.

But, despite all of the above and different types of training regimens out there, I wanted to see if Arnold's quote was accurate. What I found was, there is a plethora of research out there and it appears that just like there are different types of diets for different types of people, there really isn't a one-size-fits-all training regimen for people.

One consistent thing I did find was that when you do train with weights and even use your own body weight as the resistance, your body is subjected to micro trauma. This might sound terrible, but it's actually a healthy process. The micro traumas are essentially microscopic tears, called cataboims, in the muscle fibers, that allow them to then grow and to initiate a sophisticated metabolic process that repairs the damaged tissue beyond previous levels of density and strength; this is called anabolism. When your muscles grow, your body is conditioned to produce hormones like human growth hormone (hGH) and testosterone, which, in turn, help maintain your muscle mass, which then helps you stay lean and healthy.

Both men and women have the same catabolic-anabolic reaction; it's just that men produce testosterone at a much higher rate, and that is one main reason why men can gain muscle at a much higher rate as well. You see, even the body responds to small gains to grow.[2]

After sorting through dozens of articles and studies, I decided to interview former Olympic and strength and conditioning trainer coach and inductee to the National Fitness Hall of Fame, John Abdo. John has trained dozens of athletes, including current UFC Heavyweight Champion and five-time World Jiu-Jitsu Champion Fabricio Werdum. I asked John what his thoughts are on Arnold's quote, as it also relates to a "5 Percent More" lifestyle, and this is what he said:

> Any muscle growth is a direct reflection of physical activity exertion such as lifting weights in the gym. But Arnold is right, the last few reps, that little extra effort both mentally and physically, are what separate elite fitness athletes from weekend warriors. Forcing out more reps requires stronger mental-nerve sending signals to the muscle tissues; this is the only way muscles contract; it's called "innervation," or when a nerve stimulates a muscle to contract. It's like a wire that's charged with more electricity, or voltage, that illuminates a light bulb to burn brighter.

John went on to say, "Long-term muscle growth ensues at the end of each exercise set beyond the point where most people get fatigued, or simply give up. By pushing through this threshold, ever so slightly, on a consistent basis, long-term health benefits are exhibited, from weight loss to stronger bones to even mental health."

Take it from the most successful bodybuilder of all time, Arnold Schwarzenegger, and former Olympic trainer John Abdo, that little extra effort is what really counts. It's the epitome of the "No Pain, No Gain" mantra, and, of course, 5 Percent More.

5 PERCENT MORE STEPS AT A TIME

About six weeks ago I got a pedometer. I got it because my daughter wanted one and I thought it would help make me more accountable with regard to my movement and exercise. I go to the gym six days a week, I have always done cardio, use free weights, cross-fit routines, I even practice yoga, so even though I'm a big guy I am pretty active. I recently I turned 40 and despite my positive attitude and outlook on life, it is a fact as you get older that it does become just a little bit harder to lose weight and maintain your fitness level. So I decided to really start thinking more about how much I am actually moving. I didn't obsess over it, but I wore my device and paid attention to it throughout the day. I also was aware when I didn't wear it and how that impacted my reported overall movement at the end of each week. For instance, there were entire days when I was on a boat or at the beach or when I left the pedometer on the charger, which didn't register steps. But I knew my baseline steps my first week. My baseline was 71,000 steps, which is roughly 33 miles during the week. My second and third week, my numbers took a dip due to the fact that I was not wearing my device because it was either not possible or I just forgot. But for purposes of this exercise I adjusted the number up, knowing that I was not slacking. In fact, the third week I needed to buy a new pair of sneakers. My second week was roughly 75,000 steps adjusted, which is only about 34 miles. My third week adjusted for not wearing was slightly higher, at 82,000 steps. An interesting thing happened at the end of week three. I had a goal of

100,000 steps a week, so I knew if I wanted to actually register those steps, not only did I have to actually walk the walk so to speak, but I had to wear my pedometer. My fourth week, I jumped to 90,000 steps, which is 42 miles. Now, I was acutely aware and pushing myself just a little bit more each day. My fifth week, I broke 100,000 steps, which is roughly 47 miles. As I broke down each day, I tried to do a little more than my previous walks. But it didn't always happen. However, I was aware it didn't happen and wanted to do more, as one of my other goals was 50 miles a week. Some of you may want to call the adjustment BS and I don't blame you. But I know what I did and I also had my girlfriend as my walking partner almost every time, so she knows when I was walking and when I wasn't. Regardless, the story serves a purpose.

When I reached the 100,000 steps, it was not a complete shock to my body. I actually did it with ease, as I slowly did it over time. I also had plenty of energy and I will attempt to do more due to my goal. The devices, which are reasonably priced, helped make me accountable. The day I broke 100,000 steps, I knew I was going to be on the boat all day. So I woke up early and got 12,000 steps in before we went on the boat. But I also knew I was going to need about 5,000 more. We ordered out and, rather than having it delivered, my daughter and I walked to pick up our order.

So in order to achieve your 5 percent goals, use a partner to help make you accountable when it makes sense and use technology when necessary. I know 5 Percent More works. I do it every day and apply it to my own life in new ways to get more out of myself and life.

CHAPTER 7

Be 5 Percent Healthier

Now, we all hear stories like this every day, but this is one that is worth being told. I have been going to the same gym for years, and usually see the same people day in and day out. I always see this one guy named Mike. He's small in stature, about five-foot seven, and *was* about 230 pounds. But I have noticed him progressively getting leaner, fitter, and dropping pounds by the dozens. What was even more remarkable is that his gym routine looked about the same throughout his transformation. He works out only at lunch-time and sticks to the same routine he has been doing since I first met him several years ago, so I asked him what he did differently to bring about this remarkable change. Now, diet and nutrition are different for everybody, and some things work for some people and not others, but I still wanted to know what his formula was. When I asked him what he changed, he said it was so simple and easy. He said he stopped drinking soda and cut out ice cream. I said, "That's it?" He said, "Well, I have also cut out bread, but not all the time, just being aware of it."

In four months he lost 50 pounds by making a relatively small change in his habits. Now, this wasn't the first time I observed this simple phenomenon occur. I see this and hear stories like this all the time. Now step back, look at your diet and exercise program, if you have one, and make some slight minor changes. They can yield huge results. But you simply need to apply all the ideas of 5 Percent More that we have discussed thus far in the book to your exercise and diet routine. You have to give a little more effort, but also be willing to think a little bit differently about how to eat and exercise. The point is to adjust to something that works for you but will create a different result. That little bit of a different result over time will create huge changes if you stick with it. Like water cutting through a mountain over millions of years, your simple changes to your diet and exercise routine could cut away those pounds. And it will not take millions of years. In fact, it will happen amazingly fast.

In my business, we primarily sell health and wellness products, and, more specifically, dietary supplements. Throughout the years we have discovered that despite the plethora of information at people's fingertips about health and wellness, most people, especially Americans, are looking for a quick fix—the magic pill that can cure all disease and make you fit, beautiful, and young. Well, we don't try to push that message. Instead, we simply try to find and develop preventive products that will make a difference in your life and give you a better life in some way. And then we produce real, honest, and effective videos sharing the information that we have found and the products that we have developed. And, believe it or not, there are some amazing supplements that can help in virtually every aspect of your life. They are not the end-all, be-all, but they can help get you started.

Yet despite my company's ability to educate millions of people day in and day out, most will not ever do anything about their health until it's too late. Many will wait until symptoms arise, and then try to find a fix. The challenge is, many times that is when it is too late to make a little difference that could go a long way. So, what are we to do? Americans want the magic potion, but they don't want to have to change their lifestyle. They don't want to give up the sugary foods, the smoking, the processed foods. But we all know we are killing ourselves with our habits.

So I have been fortunate enough to have discovered products that are so simple they take only about 5 percent effort to implement in your life. They don't work for everyone, but they work for many. Sometimes they are a fast, almost instant, fix; sometimes they take time. But it's the effort of actually listening to our videos, doing a little bit of research on your own so you can prove for yourself that what we are saying is true, and then actually ordering and taking the products. A small mental and physical effort to actually take a supplement can change your life. So whether you take my supplements or others, it's the small act of actually doing it each day that makes the difference in your health.

MEDITATION

There are 1,440 minutes in a day and, as I mentioned earlier, 5 percent of that is 72 minutes. What if you focused half of that or even less on your health and wellness? What if I could show you that just 20 minutes a day of quiet time could increase your cognitive function, reduce your risk of heart disease and cancer, alleviate the silent killer of stress, help with addiction, and many other benefits. Would you do it? Would you take 1.5 percent of a 24-hour day to improve your health and wellness?

Several months ago I found transcendental meditation, also known as TM. I was sleep deprived, suffering from panic attacks, not eating like I should, and just miserable. Doesn't make any sense; I have a great life. I have great friends, great family, I can do what I want when I want, but something was off. After I suffered a panic attack that literally crippled me one night, I decided something had to change and I signed up for TM. Oddly enough, I heard of TM through listening to Howard Stern. He has discussed it several times on his show, and many other successful people in the public eye like Howard Stern practice TM. Howard told a story about his mother and how she was suicidal and found TM. Howard is a legendary neurotic and slightly OCD type-A personality, and he has said that TM has helped him manage those issues. When I began to research

TM, what really captured my attention was the science: Close to 800 published studies with almost 400 of them peer reviewed and published in some of the most respected journals.

I was talking with one of the executives at TM.org and he said that one of their biggest challenges is overcoming the stereotype that TM or meditation in general has some sort of religious element to it and that only hippies meditate. Both are false. Meditation is a way to calm one's mind, to shut down, and, essentially, reboot. Another incorrect assumption is that meditation takes years of practice in order to achieve the desired results. You can reap the benefits on day one!! There are several forms of meditation, from mindfulness to visualization to TM. I happen to practice TM, but any form is going to have a positive benefit.

A study published in 2010 in the journal *Consciousness and Cognition* that looked at the mindfulness technique found that in as little as four days of practicing this technique for only 20 minutes a day, one's cognitive skills improved significantly more than that of the control group. The study ended up with 49 volunteers who were split into two groups. One group meditated while the other was read to aloud. Both groups were put through a battery of cognitive tests prior to beginning the study. The group that meditated shocked the researchers. In one test, the meditation group performed 10 times better than the listening group.[1]

What about that silent killer, *stress*? Now, I tell people that I tend to thrive on stress, but the micro injuries it causes every day eventually catch up to people. Fortunately, I am able to recognize this and try to do something about it now. The research on stress as it relates to TM and my personal experience makes me want to get up on the rooftops and scream about the benefits. When I meditate, I can only describe what I feel as blissful nothingness. Thoughts do come in and out of my head, but I was taught that those thoughts are a part of the process of relieving stress, and it works.

In a more recent study published in the *Journal of Psycho-neuroendocrinology*, researchers found that adult patients practicing mindfulness meditation for just 25 minutes a day were able to participate more effectively in stressful math and speech tests.[2] More interestingly, not only did they report that they were less stressed, their bodies also showed it by their level of cortisol, commonly known as the stress hormone. Their cortisol levels substantiated that in less than 5 percent of their overall waking day, they were able to reduce stress and perform at a higher level.

Like I said above, what really intrigued me about TM is the science behind this particular type of meditation. When we talk about stress and what it does to the body, it is sometimes difficult to understand that stress does have a physical manifestation. Many times people associate stress with heart attacks, heart disease, and strokes. A study that was published by the American Heart Association in 2012 showed that those who had coronary heart disease and practiced TM had a 48 percent reduction in mortality, heart attack, and stroke compared to the control group.[3] So just 20 minutes twice a day—a fraction of your overall day—can do so many things for you. I just happen to be an advocate of TM, but you can try any form of meditation and it will benefit you in so many ways.

SMALL THINGS GO A LONG WAY

A little while ago I was late for a massage. I was contemplating just blowing it off because I was late, but knew I was going to get charged regardless. So I showed up 15 minutes late. When I was finally on the massage table, I apologized for being late and she said, "Better to get a massage than not to get one." I said, "Yeah, I agree." Then she said something amazing. She said, "You know, 'small things' go a long way." I said, "I couldn't agree more."

I didn't tell her about my book, but I just listened to her. She went on to tell me how she has been a massage therapist for 18 years, and knows more about the human body than most. She said even though my 50-minute massage was now cut to 20, there would still be big benefits. She said that when you get a massage, your lymphatic system is engaged and begins to flush out toxins. She said that during a massage, your muscles obviously relax and release tension. She said every touch, even for only a short period of time, stimulates blood flow throughout your body and is great not only for circulation but for your brain.

Getting more blood and oxygen flowing more efficiently will have huge long-term benefits. She then went on to say how expensive it is at the spa I was at, but that most people didn't realize that if they saw a private practitioner, even for as little as 15 minutes for a chair massage, it could be as little as 20 dollars. She ended by saying that 15 minutes and $20 once a month could increase your life span and your quality of life.

Now, I'm a proponent of massages and get them all the time, so I see the first-hand benefits from tension to stress relief. But I wanted to see if the scientific community agreed, and this is exactly what I found. Just like the science behind building muscle, there is a significant amount of research espousing the benefits of massage therapy.

In a study titled "Research shows benefits of massage therapy," researchers found that massage therapy improved "general blood flow and easing muscle soreness after exercise." Pretty obvious conclusion; I think we all realize that. But out of your overall day or week, it's such a small amount of time. More important, this study also found that massage therapy also improved vascular function (blood flow) in people who had not exercised. The improved blood flow was sustained over a period of a few days, "suggests[ing] that massage may be protective" and ultimately have long-term benefits.[4]

What if you have an existing ailment, like osteoarthritis? A recent study found that a 60-minute "dose" of Swedish massage therapy delivered once a week for pain due to osteoarthritis of the knee was both optimal and practical; at just eight weeks, participants in the 60-minute massage groups (both once and twice per week) had significant improvements in pain, function, and global response compared with participants in the usual care group. The researchers noted that there is promising potential for the use of massage therapy for osteoarthritis of the knee.[5]

What about chronic back pain? Again, this is another physical challenge that millions of Americans are plagued with. In a study conducted at the University of Kentucky, 54 percent of the people reported a meaningful decrease in pain. Researchers are very excited about these results and believe that massage therapy could lessen and even possibly eliminate the need for using highly addictive opioids.[6]

Now, many of you may be reading this and saying to yourself that you don't have the time or the money to get massages once a week. To those of you, I say that is bologna. However, I still have the answer for you, and that is to have a spouse or family member give you a massage once in a while, and you return the favor. Are they being conducted by a licensed clinical massage therapist? No. But chances of you injuring each other are very low, and small things go a long way.

One More Rep

When I was about nine years old, I was into my second season of football. Every week we had a few days of practice and then the games on the weekend. The practices weren't always the most fun, but they served their purpose, and I should not need to elaborate on that. However, one practice more than 30 years ago still sticks out like it was yesterday. It was the beginning of practice when we were warming up. We were stretching and getting our bodies ready for practice. It was early August, so it was hot, mosquitos were everywhere, and I remember just wanting to be done. Unfortunately, it was just the warm-ups. At the end of each stretching session we would do leg lifts. They are designed to strengthen your core. You lift your legs in the air then bring them about six inches from the ground. Then you spread your legs when they are about six inches from the ground. But you never let your legs touch the ground. I remember one practice when the captain, another nine-year-old, was yelling out the commands and counting the repetitions we were doing. We would generally do sets of ten, and two to three sets. This particular day, for whatever reason, the captain was pushing us harder—not the coach, but another nine-year-old. We got to the tenth set of ten and some of the boys were crying, and one boy actually puked. But the captain kept pushing us to do one more rep and one more set, mercilessly. I'm not sure if the coach was even aware, because he was over talking to the cheerleading coach. Eventually, he came back and we began the practice. The kids complained to the coach but he wasn't really listening and was now more focused on getting through the drills that he had planned for practice. The next practice, just before practice I overheard a mother yelling at the coach and telling him that it was inappropriate what the captain did, and her son quit the team. To be honest, I didn't like it either, but I stuck it out.

But here's the punchline of this little tale. That year we won every game! And the kid whose mother complained never got to feel what it was like to win. The captain went on to great things. He was a star athlete, even had a couple of tryouts for major league baseball, and is now a well-respected and successful private investigator with a happy family, and he plays competitive softball.

There are several takeaways from this story. The first is, let your kids experience adversity and hardship; it builds character. If you think that letting your kids win every game or mandating that they play every game just because we don't want to hurt anybody's feelings is a good thing, you are wrong. This is happening all over our country now, and it needs to stop. I'm not talking about five- and six-year-olds or even seven-year-olds. But there comes a point in a person's life when they have to learn how to win, how to persevere, how to work through adversity, and how to be coached. Team sports is where a lot of that happens.

Another takeaway is being able to push through one more repetition, one more set, and being able to do it without complaining has tremendous value to it. This is, again, another character-building movement, a 5 Percent More moment, that will shape a person's life, at any stage in life. Like Nike said: "Just shut up, and *Do It*!" (I added the "shut up" part.)

Smile 5 Percent More

Last week I got a call from a plastic surgeon from Tampa. He was in the process of finishing his latest book about smiling and how smiling affects your overall health. It makes me laugh and smile just thinking about the last sentence. Imagine something as simple as smiling having an impact on your health . . . really? He called me because we wanted a reference for a marketing company that I used to promote my book. We talked for a while about the publishing world. I told him about 5 Percent More, and he got so excited. He told me about how his book is designed to get people simply to smile more. He went on to talk about the research as it relates to smiling and, lo and behold, it's out there—clinical studies about how smiling can actually increase your white blood cells, can release endorphins, lower the stress hormone cortisol, and even increase your lifespan! Even "fake smiling" can help, he says. We talked about how your brain many times can't differentiate the type of stimulus but it has the same response. So why don't you start by smiling 5 Percent More each day? It's so simple but yet so effective.

CHAPTER 8

Be 5 Percent Happier

I have a close friend whom I have worked with, owned businesses with, and now employ who was forced to change his attitude ever so slightly. But how he was forced is something most people want to avoid. My friend is extremely smart, charismatic, witty, and a good guy to talk to. But a few years ago, when his business was on the rise, he began to get caught up in the ascension by drinking too much and doing drugs. He had everything: a $100,000 Range Rover for his girlfriend and a 750 BMW for himself, two houses, and the ability to do anything he wanted. He became caught up in the materialistic part of success and wasn't paying attention to his business or his own personal set of values.

Prior to this, he was never really someone who cared that much about flashy cars or weekend trips to Paris. He was very simple, had a good sense of what he needed, and was happy to have the things he had. But somehow it all went to his head and he got caught up in everything that really didn't matter. All that led to a whole lot of bad things. During his business growth, his personal life was crashing. He got arrested twice for driving under the influence, and the second time he had so many drugs on him, some of them most people never even heard of! Finally, he was sent to jail.

It was in jail where his attitude had to change or he wouldn't have survived. He did, little by little each day he was in there, reminding himself what was really important in life. From the most basic things, such as personal health and mental health to truly appreciating life as a whole, he had a 5 Percent More transformation in thought. After jail, he lost everything. He lost his license to drive, he lost the cars, he was forced to declare bankruptcy, and things only got worse, or so it seemed.

We talked a lot after he got out about his losses, and I was amazed at how he didn't look at the fall as a bad experience by that time, but rather as an awakening of sorts. He had slightly changed his mental state to realize that he still had his primary house, thankfully his health was good, and he had his girlfriend. He went back to what worked for him, and what got him to where he was before the drugs and alcohol, caring less about the material things and the business conquests and more about appreciating what he now had, and truly became self-aware.

Self-awareness is a trait that too many people lack, but it is so easy to pay attention to and make adjustments. After losing his freedom and many personal possessions, my friend was really left with no choice but to step back and take a long, hard look at where he was and where he wanted to go. I look at people every day and their inability to take stock in their own behavior and wonder if they were to just ever so slightly change what they were doing, how that could change everything.

This isn't reprogramming your mind, or going to Yoga and meditating every day, and washing those down with a mind-altering drug; this is just a simple, easy, and effective way to change your life by becoming maybe just 5 Percent More self aware each day. Think about what you will have learned about yourself after a year or a lifetime then.

The aforementioned friend is now working for me doing what he loves. He's not killing it, but he is making more money than most people, and he is happy and slowly rebuilding. And he is a wonderful reminder that people always like to blame everyone else for why they aren't happy or why they aren't where they want to be, but before you look at others, look at yourself and look at the self-imposed prison you have sentenced yourself to with that type of thinking. Really look and ask the hard questions that no one is asking you, and find the correct answers. Stop lying, stop making excuses, and become aware of your own personal behavior and habits and change them before someone or something forces you to.

Dan Harris wrote the book *10% Happier*, and I would recommend it. It is a great book about a man in the national spotlight who completely breaks down and tries to find his way. It's not necessarily about finding happiness, rather about Dan Harris trying to become grounded.

What I have found is that many of us aren't happy for a lot of reasons. But one very interesting reason why we are always chasing "happiness" is that at some point in our lives we may have peaked and reached the pinnacle, and we know it. Take, for instance, a professional athlete who retires and no longer feels the high of walking into a stadium filled with 80,000 fans and all of them clapping for him. Michael Strahan said in an interview about NFL players trying to find happiness that nothing will ever replace the feeling of sacking the quarterback in the Super Bowl, a high that is incomprehensible to many of us. Many have speculated that the reason why Junior Seau killed himself was that he was trying to chase or find the happiness he felt when he was adored by tens of thousands of fans every Sunday. Sounds crazy that he was happy in such a violent game, but football defined him. Now, there was also some brain damage caused by the violent nature of the game, but he was no doubt happy when he was on the field. As soon as he stopped playing, he lost that feeling.

EXPAND YOUR HAPPINESS HORIZONS

Every professional athlete would agree and pretty much anyone would agree that you most likely will not hit the high you hit years ago, so getting 100 percent of what you had before is many times impossible. In other words, once you walk off the field for the last time, that is it. You will never experience that feeling again. Most of us never come close to that type of high. Or do we?

What about the high school athlete who achieves amazing success but it ends there? And what of the star basketball player who isn't good enough to play Division 1, or maybe who plays at a smaller school with less acclaim. What are they supposed to do? How do they get that feeling back? Many turn to drugs and alcohol in search of the euphoric high they once felt. But getting the feeling, just 5 percent of that feeling, can be achieved. You may never walk onto that proverbial field of glory again (whatever your field was), or be hoisted into the air by an elated crowd of your peers after hitting the winning shot in the basketball state championship, or scoring the biggest win of your career, but you can achieve the feeling of happiness or success with another activity or combining multiple activities.

An interesting fact about pleasure and the feeling of happiness is that the brain actually doesn't separate or care where the pleasure comes from. Meaning, your brain will experience the same chemical reaction if you just won the Super Bowl or closed a big sale or had a great workout session. And maybe, just maybe, you can get close to that high that you once felt by spreading out your successes. From the simple act of going to the gym or cleaning the house or finishing a task at work, or completing those plans for a bathroom remodel. All of those compounded will come close to that feeling.

So when your life transitions into the next phase, take stock in the fact that you are now in a different place, and happiness can in fact be achieved through small experiences that eventually compound into a larger or greater phase of your life. Don't forget what I mentioned earlier: Smile 5 Percent More, because your brain can't tell you are faking your smile and it still releases happiness chemicals. So simple, yet so effective.

THE TOP DOESN'T MEAN YOU WILL FALL OFF—RECOGNIZE YOUR 5 PERCENT MOMENTS

A while ago I posted a picture of a man sitting on top of a mountain, and I think I said something like "climb higher" in the caption. Someone pointed out that there was nowhere else to climb. It made me laugh that they couldn't see the rest of the picture. The picture showed a man on a peak of just one mountain surrounded by hundreds of other peaks. I knew a kid in high school who was the classic popular jock. He was a three-sport captain and all-star in each sport. He set and broke every rushing record for football and points for hockey. He was on top of the world. Everyone wanted to be around him. After high school, things did not go as well in college. His grades were not so great in high school so he went to a small Division III school where he just played football. In his freshman year, he broke every Division III rushing record for the school and the conference. Unfortunately, his grades were still not where they needed to be and he eventually flunked out. That day, his life seemed to change forever for the worse. He is now a laborer who barely gets by, he is an alcoholic, and, when you look into his eyes, there is nothing there—just emptiness.

Now, this isn't always the story; you have many young kids who get to the top in elementary school, high school, college, then even the professional level. They thrive and do well at each level, because they work just a little bit harder and they are just a little bit better than the rest. But when the level ends and they are onto the next phase, they are forced to build or rebuild again. At each stage in life, we are just getting to the peak, then the next peak, and the next one. When you get to the top, it doesn't mean it's the end, it's just time to climb a different peak, to slowly build the next phase in your life. And, like the football player mentioned above, many times we get knocked off the peak, but it doesn't mean you can't climb back up that same peak or another one.

In life, we have small wins and small loses every day. Recognize them for what they are—micro moments in the macro moments of your life. Breaking your life down into these finite moments puts your entire life into perspective. I call them 5 percent moments— small events in your day-to-day life that, when built upon or learned from, make us great.

Are there big events, tragic ones, and triumphant ones in our lives? Absolutely. But, other than a freak accident, most triumphant and tragic events are a compilation of smaller events that meet a climax. But it's the 5 percent moments that ultimately determine your life's trajectory.

CARPE DIEM

I was walking into my home today with my daughter, Morgan, and she saw a little rock in our garden that had the phrase "Carpe Diem" written on it. She asked me what it meant. So I gave her the literal translation of "seize the day" or "seize the moment." But I went on to tell her that what it really means is, appreciate the smaller things in life. I told her that "Carpe Diem" is there right by our front door to remind me every day to appreciate everything I have and the loved ones around me. Then I continued and told her "Carpe Diem" reminds me to appreciate the air we breathe, the water we drink, the food we eat, the sun, the moon, the flowers, the grass, the birds.

She pretty much had enough of my attempt of explaining life to her, but I think she got it. Appreciate everything you have just a little bit more, from your family all the way down to the ground you walk on. It sounds so idealistic and ridiculous, and sometimes it is, especially when you're having trouble paying your bills, your health is poor, you have family problems, and life just seems to suck. I've been there, and when I began to realize how lucky we were, and slowly started to appreciate things just a little bit more, I got a little bit happier. Does it work all the time? Is every day sun and rainbows? Absolutely not. Do I forget to appreciate all I have? Absolutely. I'm human, just like you. But being able to recognize and appreciate life is a key part of being able to make your life even better, and the value of life is what so many people miss.

One last thing I said to my daughter. I told her, "I didn't see, hear, or become aware of the phrase 'Carpe Diem' until I was 35." I looked at her and said, "You are pretty lucky; you just learned it at nine."

Maybe you have heard this phrase, maybe you haven't. Regardless, appreciate the smaller things each day and it begins to compound and you will eventually become happier as a whole without realizing it. You see, if you are unhappy now, and if I were to tell you to make a wholesale transformation and just freakin' be happy, that would be absurd. You know why? Because it doesn't work!! But if you slowly become more appreciative each and every day, your mind-set does change. Your brain chemistry actually changes when you consciously do positive things like being thankful for being alive. So I say to you, "Carpe Diem." Don't just seize the day, seize the moments of each and every day and become self aware of when you aren't appreciative.

'NAKED AND AFRAID'

One of my guilty pleasures is reality television. I will watch pretty much any type of reality television, from *Gold Rush* to *Wicked Tuna* to *The Real Housewives*. The funny thing is that, of course, most of these do not reflect actual reality at all. But they do give us all a very interesting glimpse into the human psyche, albeit a very exaggerated and dramatic version of it. Regardless, that still can teach us something about that psyche. Well, my new favorite reality

show is *Naked and Afraid.* On this show, two strangers, one male
and one female, are dropped in some desolate area completely
naked, for 21 days. Their main and only objective is to survive. The
people on the show usually have some sort of training and background in survival. It is the ultimate test of mind and body.

These people are many times on the verge of dehydration and
starvation to the point of organ failure. They hunt for food, attempt
to start fires, drink water that is contaminated, eat bugs for protein,
battle insects that would drive anyone crazy. They all rapidly lose
weight, and as a result their mind begins to play tricks on them. It is
totally absurd that people would do this. There is no prize, no fame
really involved; it is a 21-day test.

In the episode I was watching last night, the male participant
was a 50-something former drug addict–turned-survivalist. He and
his partner were struggling to find drinkable water and a way to
purify it. They were in the Gulf of Mexico with temperatures rising
above 100 degrees. The male participant was having a difficult
time; he said that this experience was the hardest thing he had ever
done, including kicking an opioid and alcohol addiction. He took a
risk and drank some water that had bacteria in it, causing an almost
immediate case of diarrhea and stomach cramping. The show
videos their experiences twenty-four hours a day, and one night
after drinking dirty water he was absolutely miserable. It was
raining all night, he was suffering with a high fever, and bugs
the size of small birds were attacking them while he was completely
dehydrated due to the diarrhea and lack of any clean water to drink.

Every contestant can tap out, meaning they can give up if it
becomes too much to handle. But giving up leaves their partner
alone and exposed. Most contestants battle through and it's rare
that someone gives up. The next morning, the male contestant was
sitting on the beach and told the producers that he wanted out. He
couldn't take it anymore, and he needed to go home. He discussed
it with his female partner, and she understood. But she asked him

to tough it out just a little bit more to help build her shelter before he left. He agreed to battle through the day and build the shelter. The day went on; minutes and hours went by. While building the shelter, he found a bushel of bananas and other fortification. Finding this sustenance improved his spirits and his partner's. He made it to the evening and stayed the night. The next day, he was still miserable but not as bad as the day before. Whatever bug was in the water seemed to have passed.

All of this happened around days five and six of a 21-day adventure. They both, ultimately, made it through this crazy challenge. The male partner said something that resonated with me. He looked into the camera and told the audience that he was going to give the challenge one more minute and then another minute and so on. He said that anybody can do anything for one minute, and that's how he got through what many call a spiritual experience. One minute to the next to the next until the day is over, and start again. If he had thought about the two weeks he had ahead of him and the daunting task of finding food, maintaining a fire, finding drinkable water, building the shelter, fighting bird-sized mosquitoes, avoiding poisonous snakes day in and day out, he most likely would have tapped out. He broke his day down to small increments knowing that he could do anything that was thrown at him for one minute, and just built on his success. No matter how big of a task you have in front of you, the best way to approach it is one small step at a time.

YOUR TUNES, YOUR WHEELS, AND YOUR CLOTHES

I dated this girl during law school who was a great girl. I loved her and always wanted the best for her, but at the end of the day it wasn't meant to be. We lived together in a small but nice one-bedroom apartment, and it became clear that our relationship was coming to an end. I was still pretty poor, and didn't have much. When I was moving my stuff out, my dad was helping me. When we finally packed up his truck with my belongings, I was reflecting on the things I left behind and what went wrong in our relationship.

He explained to me how life works, and that I was actually lucky to have had a loving though tumultuous relationship. Then we got into the material things. We had spent practically all my student loan money to furnish the apartment, we had some pet birds and other things. I was explaining to him how much all that stuff costs. That's when he put his arm on my shoulder in front of my now old apartment and told me that all I really needed was my tunes, my wheels, and my clothes, and that everything else was replaceable. I literally laughed out loud and just looked at him in disbelief. He told me he had had his fair share of breakups, and that all you need are those three things when the relationship ends. Now, he's a product of the sixties so I had a vision of him walking out of his ex-girlfriend's with his vinyl records of Led Zeppelin, the Eagles, the Doors, and Hendrix in tow, with his long hair, and loading them into his blue 1967 Chevy Camaro, lighting up a joint, spinning the tires, and heading for the next adventure. Seems so simple, almost too simple.

But my father has said to me that he doesn't need a lot to make him happy, and he actually appreciates the simple pleasures in life. We are two different people and I want more things, the world has changed, we are from different generations, but what he was really saying is that you can take away most things that we all have, that we only need a few things to make us happy. Tunes, wheels, and clothes are not necessities to life. But they were three basic things that made him happy. He learned to appreciate them. He learned to appreciate each album, and take great pride and care of his cars. Clothes for him are more of a utility rather than a fashion statement. But the point here is, appreciate the small things, the basic things that can make you happy with or without more, and savor them. It's usually only a few things that truly make you happy. Once you can learn to appreciate the smaller things, the 5 percent things, then you can compound on more. Find your 5 percent things, then build on more.

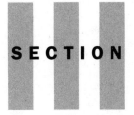

SECTION

Give 5 Percent More to Others

CHAPTER **9**

Give 5 Percent More to the People You Work With

When I was first hired as a lawyer for the company I was working for while in law school, it was my dream job, but it didn't stop me from not just dreaming about but shooting for the moon when it came to my starting salary. I asked for $98,000 a year, which was not completely unreasonable considering the market and where we were geographically located but it was definitely a stretch. It was 2004 and the economy was strong, but the competition was fierce. They ultimately hired me at a starting salary of $65,000 a year.

I was ecstatic to not only get hired but to be getting paid a decent salary. But I quickly discovered that it was not what they were giving me that made me a success, rather it was what I was able to give them. They needed me a whole lot more than I realized. In fact, had I known just how much I probably would have asked for even more than I did!

Before I got hired I knew that the company had some legal challenges, but it was much worse than I had thought. Literally the day I started in 2004, the company was sued by the Federal Trade Commission (FTC). The FTC was alleging that the company and its owners were basically criminal charlatans deceiving the American public. The FTC moved to freeze all of the company's assets and force the company into a receivership. They were basically moving to put the company out of business.

As a young lawyer I was petrified! I didn't even have my actual bar card, which is the card that a lawyer shows others to prove he is admitted to practice law. I remember saying to myself, "What did I get myself into?" I was broke but eager to work, and now the company that I took a job from was in imminent danger of being shut down by the federal government. When you have yet to actually practice law, and your first experience is fighting, literally, for your own livelihood and the livelihood of hundreds of people as your first real-world legal experience, the term "being thrown in the fire" is an understatement. I was in legal hell. It did not look good and I vividly remember walking into the CFO's office and asking him to make sure my paycheck—what was probably going to be my only paycheck—got funded. The government moved for an ex parte temporary restraining order. What this means is the government moved essentially in secret without our knowledge. They lost that first round, but we were then given only 10 days to fight for our lives.

SUCCESS IS THE DIRECT RESULT OF YOUR RESPONSIBILITY TO OTHERS

As I began to investigate on my own, I realized that we could certainly mount a defense. The challenge was that I was so green: The only thing I could really do was work harder than most would work. I went above and beyond a 5 percent effort by most work standards; however, I realized very quickly that lawyers, especially litigators, work long hours. I dove in and interviewed employees, I learned how the business operated, literally every aspect from fulfillment to accounting. I read all of the pleadings multiple times until I knew the allegations by heart. I really didn't know exactly what I was doing, but I knew that people's lives were on the line, not just mine, and I needed to do and give more than was intended when I was originally hired.

People, good people, and their families depended on the company, and I took that very seriously. I took on this responsibility and acted as if my family would be out on the street if we lost, which, actually, we quite well may have been. If we were shut down, then these families were not going to be able to feed their families, pay their rent, or live their lives the way they were used to. I made sure that I was going to make up for my lack of experience with effort. If we lost this hearing, it was over.

The pressure and stakes could not have been higher. The FTC didn't succeed in shutting the business down but they did get a preliminary injunction (PI) against the company. A PI is, essentially, a way to rein in the company as the FTC moved forward with a case against the company. We were able to prove that we weren't this big bad company as they were alleging and to continue to operate the business. As far as I was concerned, this was a *huge* win. The case was still pending and the battle went on, but due to not only my effort but the effort of our outside counsel we were able to at least continue.

It was my first big win as a lawyer. We were able to continue to operate and to grow the business. I was also very fortunate to have outside counsel who did a lot of the heavy lifting; and also one of the partners mentored me and taught me pretty much everything I know. So it wasn't just me going against the government, but I played a very important, critical role in defending and protecting the company. I also learned from this partner what long hours really meant. I would call him at 11 or 12 o'clock at night practically every day, and he was always in his office working not just on our case but others. As I discuss throughout, he is at a high level in his career and his cases are high stakes. When you are playing in the legal game where people's lives are, literally, at stake, and both sides are stacked with extremely smart and hardworking people, many times the difference between winning and losing is to outwork them. Again, both sides are working harder than most, but at their level it is just the slight edges, maybe 5 percent, that can determine whether people live or die.

But the FTC lawsuit was just the beginning of the legal challenges the company had. My bosses were wholly inadequate to run a company of that size. One of the owners was a hardcore drug addict with sociopathic, narcissistic tendencies and the other was a former drug dealer who got his high school diploma in federal prison. This combination of leadership and tainted business practices led to the company getting sued all over the country for basic things, from breach of contract to fraud. Most of this could have been avoided if they had listened to the advice of the good people who actually worked there and actually had solid business ethics.

The more I learned about the company founders and their problems, the more I had to either commit to helping them or come up with a strategy to run for cover. I decided to stick it out. But it wasn't because I was somehow stupidly loyal or scared to leave. The reality was, as a young lawyer this was experience that most would probably pay for. Through all of this business and legal chaos I learned every aspect of the business, from the most basic level to high-level negotiations with other companies. I tell people my experiences at this company were like a book on how not to run a business. I paid attention to all of the good things that the company did and the bad things, too. The experience as a lawyer was invaluable, but for me now as a businessperson it was even more valuable. I learned many valuable business lessons.

One very big lesson I learned was to face your challenges head on. And one thing I learned not to do was to avoid them. My bosses found ways to avoid tough decisions, from letting someone go to telling a vendor they couldn't pay them. When they did this, the situation grew more tense, more complicated, and more exacerbated. I discuss this in my first book, and I call them *mental monsters.* Avoiding making decisions in business makes those decisions grow into mental monsters, and when you are tasked with making decisions daily and you avoid them, you get surrounded by mental monsters that can eat away at you. Nobody likes confrontation, nobody likes firing people, nobody likes to disappoint, but things happen, and not confronting situations like this can be fatal if not handled in a timely manner.

MY JOURNEY FROM YOUNG LAWYER TO BUSINESS OWNER WAS TAKING SHAPE

Toward the end of my previous company's existence, I was running the day-to-day operations with the help of the CFO, as the two owners and the family they had hired were inadequate. The damage was so severe and difficult to overcome that I was basically just trying to stabilize the company and pay off debts. Each day we would look at the cash received, who we owed, who was the most likely to sue, and pay down as quickly as we could. It was a bizarre situation to be in, because I actually took pride in what we built despite the early challenges. I had developed great friendships with many of the people at this company, and I knew that it was just a matter of time before it all ended. I tried at one point to sit down with the owners and show them how we could save it, but they just didn't want to hear it. I even tried to rally the remaining team members together to develop a plan to stabilize, and the owners shut me down. My bosses gave up; they never really worked that hard, but at the end they didn't work at all. They just sat back and watched it all happen. But I still wouldn't give up.

Ultimately, in late 2008 the company collapsed. It is a sad story for them but an amazing experience for me. When it was time to lay off the almost 400 people, I was the one who stood in front of the staff and told them the company was shutting down. Everyone could kind of see what was going on, but no one had really told them. I felt like, as one of the top executives, we owed it to them to look them in the eyes and tell them what was happening. I remember it like it was yesterday—while my bosses were off on their boats and Jet Skis on a beautiful summer day, we summoned all of the employees into our cafeteria and I told them it was over. I basically told them they only had a couple of weeks to live and to start their final preparations.

My bosses were off enjoying a beautiful summer day on toys they couldn't afford anymore, avoiding the inevitable. They let the mental monsters destroy them. I know for a fact that, if they had made the tough decisions, had rolled up their sleeves and worked just a little bit harder, the company would have survived. Even at the end when things were bad, we were still generating millions of dollars in revenue annually, and it could have been saved with just a little more effort from the ultimate decision makers, the owners.

But they just wouldn't commit to giving a little bit more.

CHAPTER 10

Give 5 Percent More to the People You Work For

From the very moment I began working as a lawyer, I continued to get raises, one after another. My first raise was very memorable. I was making a base of $65,000 a year, and we had just successfully defended against the FTC what would have otherwise been a fatal blow. I did most of the legal grunt work, as young lawyers do, and our outside counsel finessed it a bit. But if it was not for the hard work and effort I put in, we would have lost, without a doubt. The secretary of one of the company owners came into my office and told me I was getting a big raise because of my hard work and dedication.

She seemed so happy for me and had a big smile on her face. I was so excited. I knew that people at the top of this company made great money. They increased my pay to $85,000 a year in less than a couple months. It was such an amazing feeling. My small efforts on the level I was at gave me an almost 40 percent increase in pay.

Now, as I discussed earlier, once I realized how messed up that company was and how much the rest of the company was depending on me, I felt an obligation to my fellow employees to keep the boat afloat as long as I could.

And even as totally screwed up as my employers were at the time, I still felt a tremendous obligation to them—to make them look better—to make them weather the storm and prosper as much as I could for as long as I could. And that's what made me successful there.

Now, I have always had a good "work ethic," but I mentioned our outside counsel in the last chapter. His worth ethic at the time seemed to be so far over the top. I remember asking him why he was always in the office so late, and he said he wasn't the only one, that many lawyers were still in the office, especially opposing counsel. He would get there at 8 AM every day and sometimes not leave the office until 12 AM that night. Now, was he doing way more than the average worker in the United States workforce? Absolutely. But at his level, just like the professional athletes, he was doing just a little bit more than his colleagues. Several years later he was asked to become an equity partner at his law firm. This is one of the largest law firms in the world and his efforts have, literally, paid off.

This is where as a lawyer I realized that if I wanted to be at the top of my game, if I wanted to be really good at what I did, I needed to play in the big leagues, but slowly get there. Eventually, over time, I learned more, I grew more, and I began to actually do a lot of the stuff that the outside law firm charged us thousands of dollars for. These small, incremental learning cycles for me also paid off. I received a few more smaller raises that got me to about $100,000. But I remember the next big one was when I realized that my small efforts at the high level of corporate law were saving my company literally millions of dollars.

I was growing each day and increasing my net worth to the company not only as a lawyer but also as a businessperson. Each day I was learning more, and I was adding more value both on the legal and the business front. One time shortly before I asked for my raise, I was editing one of our call center scripts for compliance purposes. As I was editing, I realized that as a company we could double the price of one of our products and it would have no negative impact on the business. I knew this because each and every day I was learning more and more about how the overall business worked. These smaller bits of information I was learning each day were compounding in my brain, and my business savvy was growing exponentially. I notified my bosses of what I had discovered and they let me make the change. That one small change in our call center script, literally just changing a number from one to two, netted the company millions.

I confidently walked into the owner's office and explained to him how I was saving him millions of dollars in legal fees and avoiding potential legal battles and making him millions by understanding the business even better than he did (I didn't say that exactly, but conveyed that message in a more diplomatic way). I also thanked him for the opportunity he gave me; I was a young lawyer with zero experience and I was given the amazing opportunity to play in the big leagues pretty fast. If it wasn't for his faith in me, I would not be where I am today, and I have thanked him for that time and time again. And that faith was directly related to my loyalty to him and his partner, and I made sure he knew that, through both my actions and my words.

After the discussion he asked what I should be making and I said $150,000 a year. He agreed, and it was a done deal. That same year I was granted the President's Award, where an employee is recognized for his hard work and dedication, and that award came with a $10,000, net, check. I was recognized in front of the whole company and the recognition was worth more than the check. It felt really good. Toward the end I was making a little over $225,000 a year, more than all of my classmates, some of whom had an educational pedigree that was just astounding.

When you look back on my experience, think about how you, too, can apply the same things I did to your business and increase your net worth. Small changes over time had a huge impact on my professional life and can do the same for you.

THE 5 PERCENT MORE MENTALITY—WHERE DOES IT COME FROM?

When I was working those long hours, and giving what seemed at the time to be a tremendous amount of effort and work compared to the others at the level I was at, I was just doing a little bit more than them. I was certainly working a lot harder than a customer service agent at the company, but when I was a customer service agent, I did just a little bit more than all of the others, which allowed me to get to the next level. So when it seems like you are working more hours than everyone else, don't look at everyone, look at your peers and counterparts and see if you are doing just a little bit more than them. That's what separates good from great. I was always the first one there and the last one gone.

As I began to realize how important it was to give more, it became even clearer to me that my bosses weren't doing the same, and that's why they were having so many problems. That their impending failure contrasted with my success in the company even further reinforced my conviction that giving led to getting. Making money, running a business, and building a great life for yourself can make you feel great. But, deep down inside if you aren't helping others grow and reach their goals, then you will not lead a fulfilling life. One of my bosses who recently passed away was only concerned about what he got. He was only concerned about his money and he was envious of some of his employees as they grew professionally. This behavior was rooted deep in his own inferiority complexes and was a contributing factor to the company's demise. As a result of his inability to give to others around him and hoarding what he thought was only his, the company literally began to crumble. Many of his employees resented and mocked him, and then he hired people, mostly family members, who were even more inadequate than he was to manage the business. These people he hired weren't bad people, they were just not suited for the job.

So rather than making a little bit less and paying his employees just a little bit more, he opted to keep "what was his," hire incompetent people, and be surrounded with resentment.

But I kept helping. I went the extra mile to help them. The last year and a half, I was essentially trying to run the business, despite their attempts to stop me from fixing problems. It was hell! But it all led me to knowing not only how to run a company but how *not* to run a company.

When I realized the end was near, I knew my time had come. The partners were fighting. Finally, I came to them and told them that I was going to start my own company. But I still helped the bosses, even offered them both jobs.

I learned from that experience and from advice of very successful businesspeople that you must "spread the wealth" and surround yourself with people who are smarter than you. So, as you are growing and climbing the ladder of success, be sure to give back to the people around you and make sure that they are taken care of. Doing this will ensure longevity and prosperity long term.

ALWAYS GIVE MORE THAN EXPECTED

A friend of mine is a vice president of a large software company, and when I was discussing with him 5 Percent More he told me this fantastic story. He had two software engineers who had both applied for a management position. In this position, they would be in charge of projects within their division and responsible for managing a small staff. My friend told me how he had a tough time differentiating between the two. Both went to prestigious colleges, both had their master's degrees, both were real go-getters. He said that each candidate cared about his job and was the best at what he did. Both were always the first to arrive and last to leave their job. But he could only choose one.

The company offered free training courses for its employees to help them progress and improve their own net worth. One course that was offered was how to be a great manager. This course taught the skills necessary to manage and lead people, how to deal with conflict, and how to get your people to perform at a high level. The class was offered just once a week, two hours a night for six weeks. It was on the campus of the company, so the employees didn't have to go anywhere. Any employee could take the classes offered. When my friend was approaching the deadline to make the decision, he was reviewing their files and he couldn't believe what he had missed. Only one of the candidates had taken the free management course offered by the company. That candidate was the one chosen. It was a tough decision, but that candidate had done just a little bit more than his competition. He and his counterpart were both operating at the same level as far as skills, drive, and pedigree, but that 12 hours over the course of six weeks that taught him just a little bit more got him the job. My friend told me that the position came with a significant increase in pay and was a position that could certainly lead to more growth. Take a look at what level you are playing at and do just a little bit more, and you will get more.

So whether it's doing big things for the company, like saving it from disaster, or little things like taking a class to better yourself, the idea is to give more to the people you work for. That may not be the status quo or the most popular idea nowadays, but it's a tried and true idea, one that has worked for me and countless others who came before me, and will work for you, too.

CHAPTER **1 1**

Make Life 5 Percent More Exciting for Others

I was at breakfast recently and a little girl no more than three was so excited when she was going through a book and was able to identify the animals in the book. She proudly announced to her mom, "Mommy, that's a giraffe" and "Mommy, that's a panda bear." She was so excited!

But there comes a point in a child's life where their excitable expressions become muted. That's because parents are constantly hushing children, telling them to quiet down or, even worse, to shut their mouths. What if we as a society allowed that excitement to grow and expand? What if we embraced a child's excitement level?

Why do we have to suppress that excitement? What if you were 5 Percent More excited about the basic things in life? From just waking up to going to the gym, what if you perceived it all through the eyes of a child? Imagine how your work day would go if you were just a little more enthusiastic about your job. I will tell you this, if you see your life as more exciting, then your life will *be* more exciting. You will begin to appreciate the little things.

And the first step to making this happen is to allow your children to be excited and not suppress that excitement. Watch it grow and expand. And soon you will see your chance to get your excitement back through them and other children around you.

We all had it when we were kids, too, but somewhere along the way of "growing up" we lost it, and, in a way, lost ourselves. Well, here is your chance not just to get it back but to spread it to others.

And 5 Percent More excitement will translate into a more fulfilled life for everyone.

WHY ARE KIDS SO HAPPY?

You ever notice the unadulterated joy and happiness children seem to have? Long before they learn about the real world, kids, for the most part, are blissfully optimistic about pretty much everything. Yeah, they have meltdowns when they don't get the toy they wanted or they get sad when their goldfish dies, but children in general are just happier than adults.

There are so many reasons why. For instance, a child doesn't have to worry about the mortgage payment, or going to work day in and day out, or the economy crashing. They only have to be concerned with their little world of new and exciting things, and most children are just happy even when things don't work out, probably because they always have something new and exciting to look forward to. Every day is a chance to see the world of new and exciting possibilities.

I have a little girl who is now 9 and soon to be 10, and I am watching her grow so quickly. But one of the many things I learn from her is that I try to see what she sees in the world. When she sees the snow, she thinks sledding and snowmen. When we see the snow, we see shoveling it and bumper-to-bumper traffic. When we go to the grocery store, she sees watermelon and thinks about how sweet it tastes or she is anxiously anticipating that I will go to the deli to get her a piece of cheese. We see the stress of having to purchase what is needed, and get annoyed by the lines and the increasing cost of food. In the mornings, she sees another day to have fun, to learn, to grow. We, as adults, think about what needs to be done and think about our responsibilities as adults. When she goes to bed, she is dreaming about what tomorrow will bring, while we are lying down dreading tomorrow.

See, kids are lucky they haven't been poisoned yet. They have their own responsibilities and stressors just like us, and to them they are just as important as paying the mortgage, but they still skip to school and get genuinely excited when they get a lollipop at the bank. The reason for this is because of the way they think. Now, completely changing your thought process is not what this book is about; it is about those baby steps. So, start looking at the world through the eyes of a child and start enjoying the things around us just like they do.

I am not just asking you to change how you think. No, I am asking you to change how you act! Act just a little more excited about everything. Just take my word for it and do it. Just watch the kids around you—any kids around you—and do as they do.

One other thing: If you notice that your child in this techno-logically advanced day and age isn't happy, or isn't appreciating the snowflakes falling or the waves crashing or the sun shining, remind him or her of how awesome life is. Reinforce it every day by saying things like "Honey, look at the cute squirrel" or "Isn't the sun so beautiful?" or "Look at that full moon." Don't let your kids lose the excitement we are all born with.

IT'S CONTAGIOUS—TRUST ME!

Each day you will notice your mood elevated. When you feel down, you will know that maybe you haven't thought like a kid and need to start going back to it. Once you fully commit to this process, something even more amazing will happen. People around you will start telling you how your excitement is rubbing off. They will be getting a thrill out of just watching you live—the same way you got high from watching kids. And soon they will be doing it, too. That will then get you excited again just knowing that you caused it.

I've talked about how fortunate I am to have not only read Zig Ziglar's books but to be in his company many times. His personality was so infectious. He was always so upbeat and happy. When he greeted you he had a huge smile, even if he barely knew you. He genuinely cared about what you had to say. He was just happy, all the time. He told me when we were at dinner once that he loved life and loved the place that God had created, and he chose to be happy and enjoy it while he was here. It hit me pretty hard and even now I realize that many times I forget and need to get rid of what he calls "stinking thinking." Zig was and is an inspiration of mine because of the life he led and how he chose to live it.

Just recently I was in a shopping mall, and just before closing time, around 9:45 PM, I walked into a men's clothing store. I had never shopped there before but I was in a pinch and I needed a couple of dress shirts. It was dead in the store; no one was there except three salespeople. They all looked at me, but only one decided to greet me—a woman by the name of Anne. She asked me how I was doing, and I responded, "Fabulous, but I will get better." She kind of giggled and said, "Well, that is great." The other two salespeople looked up and took notice as well. Now, I happened to be coming from the gym, so I was in sweatpants and a sweatshirt, so I didn't look like the type of guy who wore dress clothes. But I obviously was. She took me around and I bought some shirts, but then I bought a bunch of other stuff. She then sold me a shirt that someone had returned. It wasn't particularly my favorite shirt, but she sold it with enthusiasm and told me what a great deal it was. I said, "Okay, I will take it," and she responded by saying, "Fabulous," with a big smile. I said, "See, now you really are fabulous." One of the other salespeople reminded her of what I said when I first walked in. I didn't spend a ton of money so she wasn't super excited about that, but now at the end of her long shift, she was feeling fabulous and I was, too—not because of my new clothes, but because I knew that my small amount of enthusiasm infected her, and it may infect others through her. I learned this technique from Zig and it works, so try it and apply it daily.

DO 5 PERCENT MORE STUFF

Once you start getting more excited about everything that you do, then you might as well start doing more. In fact, once you have that attitude you will probably want to do so much more—because you will be so excited. See how this works.

Recently I had a medical scare and, like the slightly hypochondriacal person I am, began to think about all of the things I did not do. Now, most would say that I have lived a pretty good life up until this point, and I agree. I have been all over the country, have a best-selling book, a great company, and many material things that most people only dream about, but there are so many basic things I have not done.

I have not been to the Grand Canyon; I have not gone to see the pyramids in Egypt; I have not seen my daughter graduate high school, get married, and have children. That last is the most important to me, but there are so many little things that people can do and just don't.

As I get older, like most, I get wiser and appreciate life more and more every day. Every day, try to do something new and something you have not done before. From trying a new food to maybe going to a place you have not been before. Day in and day out, we continue to live our lives, but we are, in reality, just going through the motions. We aren't living; we are just existing. Do things each day that make you happy. Even do things that actually may take you out of your comfort zone, that may not make you feel happy per se but will give you a sense of accomplishment.

If you realize how exciting life is, why not try to live and experience as much of it as possible? Why not seize the adventure at every turn—just like a child? And look forward to every new day as another opportunity to be that excited.

CHAPTER 12

Reading 5 Percent More to Our Children

There are 1,440 minutes in a day, and 5 percent of that is 72 minutes. Most elementary schools, at least the good ones, recommend children read 20 minutes a day. That's about 1.5 percent of the total minutes in a day. Well, what if you did even a little more—maybe 5 Percent More!

Why is reading to our children important? Well, the answer would seem pretty simple. Read to our children and they will do better in things such as reading comprehension, testing, social skills, communication skills, and, ultimately, life skills. A child's chances of ultimately having a better life are irrefutable if they are read to and learn how to read early on. The hard science proves what most of us already know: Reading to our children is just about the best thing we can do for them at an early age.

We are quick to think about and talk about how adding a few more dollars to our IRA or a few more dollars to our savings can really grow over time. Yet how often to we think about how a few more minutes of time with your child can compound over time? And reading is one of the best ways to make that deposit grow.

I had a chance to interview Brian Gallagher and Dr. Jean Ciborowski Fahey of Reach Out and Read, an organization founded in 1989 that distributes thousands of books for children and encourages pediatricians to stress the importance of reading. They went beyond what the empirical data shows in our interview. During the ages 0 to 5, a child's brain is the most malleable.

In other words, their brains are developing and growing faster than at any other time in their lives and can be molded by what is being put into their brains. Dr. Fahey, an early literacy expert, explained that the neural pathways in the brain grow fast during this time frame, but they grow and develop faster if children are read to.

Also known as neuroplasticity, the brain changes and evolves when information is, essentially, uploaded to the brain through our surroundings and interactions. In a study provided by Reach Out and Read, scientists stated that the single most important parental activity to prepare a child to succeed in learning to read is actually reading aloud to the child.[1] Mr. Gallagher went on to say, "Imagine if we just read to our children 5 percent more and what it would do to their long-term development and success. I don't need a study or research to tell you, they will be 5 percent better."

Science has proven that the more a child uses a particular neural pathway, the more developed and sensitive it becomes. The sad part about brain development is that the neurons actually die if not stimulated or used. The good news, however, is that despite the fact that neurons may die due to lack of use, our brains can actually grow and create new pathways even as we age. It is obviously best when a child is able to develop the neural pathways early. So the next time your child asks you to read one more page or read the story one more time, think about the long-term benefits and how much just 5 Percent More can do for your child.

5 PERCENT MORE WAYS TO READ TO YOUR CHILD—EVEN IF YOU CAN'T

What if the parents are illiterate? What if they are working three jobs and don't have 1.5 percent of time to spare? Are the children doomed? I asked Dr. Fahey what we can do. She said nothing takes the place of reading with your child, but if it truly is something that you can't do, the next best thing is to talk with your children.

Tell them stories, ask them questions, and engage with them. The more words they hear, the more they listen to how stories are told, the more their brains will be engaged and develop. Talk to your children just a little bit more and the long-term benefits are extraordinary. In 1995, Betty Hart, PhD, and Todd R. Risley, PhD, conducted a groundbreaking study in Kansas City looking at how reading and words affect our children. What they found was remarkable. Doctors Hart and Risley documented 42 children from the time they began to speak to the age of about three from those born into poverty, middle-class, and professional families. They actually sent people into the homes of these children and observed, transcribed, and recorded what was said in the home.

Most would assume, and a lot of the science substantiates the fact, that the wealthier kids are always going to be better off. But that isn't necessarily the case. The study documented some amazing facts: so many facts that the study was published in a book titled *Meaningful Differences in the Everyday Experiences of Young American Children*. What they found was more than noteworthy; for instance, in a 100-hour week (given a 14-hour waking day), the average child in a professional family was provided with 2,150 words per hour; the working class child, 1,250 words; and the poor child, 620 words[2]; that up to 98 percent[3] of a child's vocabulary consisted of words in their parents' vocabulary regardless of socioeconomic status; and that some parents used words of encouragement and expressed approval more than 40 times an hour and others only four.[4] All the data at first blush would again strengthen the popular premise that money or economics will give a child a better chance in his or her academic development. However, that popular premise is wrong. Doctors Hart and Risley stated that whatever the heredity of the children or economic situation, those children who have more experiences through verbal interaction and reading will develop the intangibles of confidence and motivation that will give them the skills needed to achieve success later on in life. In other words, the more time we spend reading with our children and, equally important, talking to them, the more they will develop. So it's not the money, it's not race, it's not ethnicity; it is quantity of time.

Imagine what our children—your children—can do if we just talk with them and read to them a little bit more, just 5 Percent More. When writing this book, I was a little hesitant at first as to whether to interview others or include scientific data because it's not really my "style." But the above data and observations are crystal clear and powerful. Just talk more to your kids, and they will have a better show of success in life.

SECTION

IV

Give 5 Percent More to Your Business

CHAPTER 13

5 Percent More Revenue

My first year in business at Blue Vase Marketing, we did more than $9 million in revenue. We started with credit cards, a little bit of cash, and valued relationships I had developed over the years. Nine million dollars in revenue is impressive considering what we started with, but the following year we doubled the number to $18 million, and our third year we did more than $30 million. Last year we did close to $50 million!

Some look at our growth and think it's amazing and fast. I think and I know it was the opposite. We slowly grew each and every department and added a little more each day, maybe 5 percent, each week, each month, so that we could grow without imploding. These small changes early on increased our productivity and our cash flow and, ultimately, increased our revenue so that we could continue to grow.

When we first started Blue Vase with just a handful of people and practically no money, we had to figure out a way to make all that happen. I mention later on my propensity for wanting to grow fast, but we didn't have the resources, so we slowly grew each week. Each week we grew our customer base, and each week we added more employees. More important, we looked at the business itself and how we could grow the business as an entity. In the beginning we didn't have our own customer service or fulfillment department. We had to use outside third parties to handle our shipping and customer service. For my business and what we do, it was not efficient or cost effective, but we didn't have the facilities or the manpower when we first started. So we made a plan to slowly build our customer service department. In our small office we had what I called our lounge area, a place for employees, including myself, to just kick back, watch TV, take a nap, etc. Well, in order to grow, that small room became our first customer service room. We started with just one person, then it became two, then three, then four, and, eventually, we pulled the customer service from the third-party company and saved our company thousands of dollars each week. It was better for our customers and made us more efficient. We essentially did the same thing with our fulfillment department. We started shipping directly out of our offices, so that we could figure out the systems and put proper processes in place. Eventually, we went from shipping just a few packages a day to now shipping thousands a day.

Just this year we built our own production studio in our building. Most of our infomercials in the past were shot in Los Angeles, which costs a lot of money. We made the decision that if we were to slowly fund a studio space while still shooting in Los Angeles, eventually our studio would be operational and save us tens of thousands of dollars each time in production and travel costs. Building a studio was expensive, and even today working capital is hard to come by, so week by week we set a little aside to buy the lights, to build the set, to soundproof, to build the radio studio, to furnish the offices, until we were ready. By doing it this way I was still able to use my production business in Los Angeles but was slowly preparing for the future and the growth of the company. Now, we are not only using the studio for ourselves but major production companies rent our studio, and it will eventually become another stream of income. Just recently we began to slowly buy our own media for some of our advertisements. This small step will eventually be a huge revenue source for us and a natural progression for a fully integrated marketing firm.

5 PERCENT INCREASES MEAN STABLE BUSINESS

I used to go to a small coffee shop/diner. They served a very unique fresh breakfast and lunch. I had gourmet coffee served in actual mugs and great sandwiches like an egg and avocado sandwich for breakfast. I used to love to go there in the morning to get my day started. It was a classic, small town, hipster coffee shop that served lunch too. I became friendly with the owner and she read my first book. One day we were talking about business and she was telling me how she worked a second job. I was shocked. I didn't know it was possible. Running a restaurant that is open six days a week takes up a lot of your time. She told me that the shop that I so loved to hang out in was probably going to close. In a selfish effort to keep my favorite place open, I suggested that she just raise the prices by—you guessed it—5 percent.

She was hesitant and didn't seem open to the idea. I explained that if people liked the food and the environment, they would pay a little more. She didn't take my advice, and to be honest I didn't really push it. Eventually my favorite place closed down. A couple of months ago, I found out that they had reopened in a very high-rent area. I went by and the place was thriving. There were people literally lined up out the door for lunch. The menu was slightly different and there was a lot more to offer. The biggest thing I noticed was the prices. Her prices were about 20 percent higher than her previous place—way more than 5 Percent More. They were higher, but the quality was the same as before and people were still coming. She most likely increased the prices to pay the rent, but ultimately to improve the bottom line and maintain solvency. Over the holiday season, I ran into the owner and she hugged me and looked at me without saying a word. Her eyes and embrace said it all. She is now in a much bigger place, with much higher prices, and also much higher revenue and profit.

Recently, I came across an article that helped crystallize the point of the above story. If you have a good product, sell the product, not the price. People will always pay more, especially just a little bit more, for a great product or service. Over the years I have been forced to raise my prices, and I was always reluctant. The salespeople pushed back, management told me I was crazy, but it was the only option we had in order to maintain our business and continue to grow. Don't be afraid to increase your prices. People will always pay more, especially if you are already adding value to their lives.

5 PERCENT MORE AT WORK

Let's assume your business is generating ten million dollars in gross revenue annually. That equals $833,333 per month. Let's also assume that you have a 7-percent profit margin on that $10 million. If you could find a way to become 5 Percent More efficient and, as a result, generate 5 Percent More revenue each month while keeping your costs relatively the same, the following year you would have close to three hundred thousand dollars more in profit. You can continue to do the math, but even if you stayed the same as month 12 for the entire third year, your profit margin continues to grow.

$833,333.00 × 1.05, or 5 Percent More, equals:

- Month 01 = $875,000
- Month 02 = $918,750
- Month 03 = $964,687
- Month 04 = $1,012,921
- Month 05 = $1,063,567
- Month 06 = $1,116,746
- Month 07 = $1,172,583

- Month 08 = $1,231,212
- Month 09 = $1,292,773
- Month 10 = $1,357,412
- Month 11 = $1,425,282
- Month 12 = $1,496,546
- Total for that year is $13,927,479

SMARTER THAN ALBERT EINSTEIN AND BETTER THAN THE DOMINO EFFECT!

I recently picked up the book *The One* by Gary Keller, and in the first few pages it refreshed my memory and understanding of geometric progression, which I learned about as general counsel of the multilevel marketing (MLM). Now, I am not a mathematician, so I will explain this mathematic principle as simply as I can. It is basically the mathematical formula by which you multiply by the same factor each time. For example, to create the sequence 1, 3, 9, 27, 81, 243, 729 and so on, I am just multiplying by the same factor—the number 3. As you can see, we went from 1 to 729 in just six steps, geometrically progressing by three. The powerful nature of this formula is how quickly you can accomplish things just by making small increases.

Discussing the domino effect, Gary Keller described a domino geometric progression: By doubling the size of the first domino, which is only two inches, by the time you get to the 57th domino it is as large as the distance from Earth to the moon. The challenge with geometric progression is that most people, and I mean *most* people, cannot double their efforts consistently time and time again. The theory is powerful and shows how small changes— increasing the last result by the same factor at each step—can have huge results, but applying it to everyday life is unrealistic and beyond the reach of most.

I first learned of the principle of geometric progression at an opportunity meeting for the MLM for which I was general counsel. The owner of the company told the crowd how Albert Einstein once said that geometric progression is the most powerful mathematical formula to have ever been discovered, but, more important, it could make people rich. An opportunity meeting is usually the first meeting when someone is recruited to come learn about the company and the opportunity of signing up. It is a sales presentation at its best. At this particular meeting, the owner was in a $2,000 custom suit, red power tie, Brioni shoes, and a solid gold Rolex. He described how the MLM worked, and it was pretty simple. All he asked was that each person sign up two people, who then sign up two people, who then sign up two people, and watch their organization grow. Some would call this a pyramid scheme, but it's actually a pyramid dream.

In MLMs, like most sales organizations, only a few people are able to do what the perfect sales pitch requires to make the real money. It isn't as sexy if someone were to get up in a room and show what a gradual 5 percent increase month after month looks like versus doubling or tripling their production. But this dream pitch is ultimately where most MLMs fail. Geometric progression may, in fact, be the most powerful mathematical formula to make you rich, but it isn't attainable and it's unrealistic when presented in a manner of progressing by multiples of two or greater. Rather, a small percentage is what is not only realistic, but also attainable, and can also make you a lot of money!!

What I am asking you to do in 5 Percent More is not to double the size of your domino so that you will be on top of the moon quickly; rather, what I am saying is, to get to the moon, don't fantasize about it. Geometric progression is just a mathematical equation to show you the power of small changes, but the examples of progressing by double or triple factors are not the recipe for success. You can't eat a whole elephant by doubling your previous bite, but you can if you slowly increase the size of your bites. A 5 percent geometric progression will yield much better results, so that what starts out as a really minor change will get you major results. But the key is consistency even when faced with adversity. When you fall short, keep at it and keep working even when it seems like it isn't working. It will. I promise.

I'M WRONG

I've studied success and experienced success at a level that most people can't comprehend. Some people at the top appear to be doing things at a pace that is beyond what the average person could even fathom. And they are. But they have compounded on their success. They didn't just get to the level they are at; they worked at getting there. There are programs and seminars out there that tell you that you need to go a hundred miles an hour at all times to get to where you want to go. These books and seminars work for a small, limited part of the world's population and usually are not able to sustain success. Do just a little bit more at each level and you will not only achieve success; you will maintain it. So when you see how a person is working hard and putting in countless hours and they have attained remarkable success, remember it didn't just happen; it was a progression.

TROUBLED PAST TO TAKING JUST ONE CLASS

I am close with a woman whom I've known for most of my life. She has struggled with addiction and anger issues throughout her life. Her childhood wasn't the best: her parents were both drug users, her neighborhood was riddled with drugs and crime, and she became a product of that environment. I've always tried to help her in any way I could. I've mentored her, given her a job, had many heart-to-heart talks with her, and encouraged her to seek counseling, but things never really got through.

Several years ago, she seemed like she was turning her life around. She had a steady job and enrolled in classes at the local community college. I was very proud of her, until she got arrested for dealing large amounts of marijuana. Needless to say, her college days were over. After a fairly lengthy legal battle, she took a plea and agreed to two years in the house of corrections at the female prison in Framingham, Massachusetts. I stayed in touch with her, wrote her, visited her, and put money in her commissary. I reminded her during her time that she was locked up to try to take advantage of the programs the jail had. But she didn't do anything to improve her life while locked up. She just did her time.

Well, after she had been out for some time she was still struggling to find her way. Again, I took her under my wing, encouraged her, and tried to steer her down the right path. Nothing seemed to work, until a few months ago when something clicked. I said, "Hey why don't you take a class? Just one class. Taking this class will challenge you and introduce you to new people and new things."

Well, she is now in just one class and excited about life. She now has vision and has enrolled in one other class in the spring. These small steps, 5 percent moments, I believe are what are really going to change the trajectory of her life. You can see it in her eyes and in her voice. Even her text messages are more positive and upbeat. One small step toward her original goal of getting her degree has now given her hope and purpose.

5 PERCENT MORE CUSTOMERS

In any business, one of the most difficult things to do is acquire customers. The next thing a business must do is to cultivate those customers. Successful businesses, the ones that have been around for a long time and will always be around, know how to do that. What I mean is, they spend more time than their competitors with their customers, from offering their customers incentives to buy more products, to just picking up the phone and saying hello.

I discussed rapport building in *Ask More, Get More*, but what really provides a solid foundation that will ensure longevity in the business world is the ability to connect and interact with one's customers. In my business, we generate thousands of leads every week. But these are actual customers, not just leads, who have decided to spend their hard-earned money on one of our products. I learned early on that staying in touch with those customers, engaging those customers, and talking with those customers have allowed us to grow and build a solid foundation. A very successful business owner told me one day that it is much smarter in business to spend a little more time with your current customers than to neglect those customers and chase leads that may never turn into customers. In business, we always need to be looking for new customers, but we also need to step back, slow down, and figure out a way to spend more time with our current customers. They have already decided to buy from you and they will most likely buy again. I could write a lot more about this concept and, in fact, I do a webinar training specifically about how to spend more time with your customers in an effort to grow.

This is not a new concept, but it is a sound business principle that totally fits into the 5 Percent More model. A little more time with your current customers will reap long-term benefits for your business.

JUST A LITTLE BIT MORE!

When being interviewed by *Forbes* magazine in 2000, Lindsay Owen-Jones, the then-CEO of L'Oréal, one of the most—if not *the* most—successful cosmetics company in the world, was asked why L'Oréal was crushing its competition, and she said, "We just love the business a little bit more than our competition."[1]

L'Oréal is at the pinnacle of cosmetics, at a level that many cosmetics companies aspire to, and, according to their leader at the time, they just loved the business a little bit more and that's what made them great. OJ, as he was referred to, ran that company for 30 years, and his success and his company's success were due to loving and caring just a little bit more than the rest. Sounds a whole lot like the 5 Percent More mentality at work to me.

CHAPTER 14

5 Percent More Profit = Being 5 Percent More Efficient and 5 Percent More Accountable at Work

I have friends from all walks of life who ask me for advice on business, and recently a really close friend of mine came to me pretty desperate. He has been working in the beverage industry for close to 20 years and has had tremendous success in the past, but his new business is struggling. We talk pretty often about his business, and right now things seem very busy with a lot of positive activity and hard work, but no results or high payoff accomplishments.

My friend's company markets, promotes, and sells products in the wine, beer, and spirits industry, and his company seems to be doing a lot of great things. He is signing new brands very frequently to promote and market, and he is constantly working. His employees all seem busy, too, but there is little revenue coming in. Why?

I always hear people talk about how they work 50 to 60 hours a week, even 70 hours a week. Most are not being honest with themselves, but my friend really was in the office five to six days a week, 10 to 12 hours a day. We were talking about how great things were, but also looking at why there was no money coming through the door. His phones were ringing, he had people calling on potential clients, he was sending out samples like crazy, but something was missing. We were candidly discussing how hard he was working with little payoff, and I was concerned not only with the business but with him personally as a great friend. He was telling me how he lives, breathes, dreams, daydreams, eats, and bleeds the company. There was no one more dedicated to his business than himself. Why then was there little revenue coming in? Why was he working so hard, why did his company seem so busy, but still he wasn't making money? He appeared to certainly be putting in the effort. So then what?

Answering these questions takes me back to the early days of my company that I described earlier. We were steadily growing, and the money kept on rolling in, but we were still struggling. We were growing but, incredibly, as we continued to grow we continued to lose more and more money. My company sells products that come in certain configurations for many reasons. Like many brands that are consumable, we like to package and sell them a certain way to increase efficiency and maximize profit, something I really didn't understand at first. There were and are many ways to package or bundle our products, but we found the most profitable is a configuration of a three-month supply, meaning if the product is designed to last for one month, we would like to sell the customer a three-month supply. This was the sweet spot for orders. They would be more likely to buy a three-month supply as the cost wasn't too high. Any smaller and we were not maximizing our profit; any larger and we found customers either wouldn't bite or would return the order because they were overwhelmed with a large box sent to them, so a three-month package was also less likely to be returned.

After about a week of meeting with my team members and accounting staff, we realized that despite our revenue we needed to sell more of these smaller configured packages, like the ones described above, as opposed to pushing for bigger orders. This was about 2012, and at this time we were millions of dollars in debt and I didn't have the resources to continue on. Right around this time I was also working with a company that had lent me millions of dollars and was working on a plan to specifically get them paid back.

Some of the plan included a layoff. I also had to reduce people's salaries and even ask some executives to skip checks.

I met with our sales team and explained to them that we needed them to change their mentality of selling a lot on the first phone call and think about the package that we as a company needed. I showed them that the smaller package made more sense long term for the company. Well, the salespeople didn't listen to me, and they kept selling bigger packages that brought in a lot of revenue, but in the long run were significantly less profitable, even though it meant a higher commission to them. Now here is the crux of the story. They were selling bigger packages and making bigger commissions. They only saw what was going into their pockets. They didn't think about next year. They only thought about their next paycheck. I was thinking about staying in business so I could actually get them more paychecks for a long time! I knew that I had to, essentially, force them to sell the smaller packages we needed in order to survive.

So I changed the compensation plan. Changing the compensation plan in any sales organization is a slippery slope. We thought about how to force them to sell the package we needed. We could have easily just removed the large package, but sometimes that package made sense for some of the customers. What we did instead was reduced the commission on the larger package and increased the commission on the smaller packages.

ONE THING THAT IS ALWAYS CONSTANT IS CHANGE

I thought the sales staff was going to lynch me. Some quit instantly. One sales agent sent me a barrage of text messages, calling me a loser, telling me I didn't know how to run a company, threatening to "call the authorities," then called me and actually told me he hoped that I died in a fiery car crash. Sounds a little drastic, right? He wouldn't let me explain that it was actually going to work. I was trying to tell him a couple of things, which included why small changes have a big impact, but also not to burn bridges. Needless to say I fired him. Incidentally, a few months ago he actually called me, and he said he wanted to have coffee with me. Now, I had heard through the grapevine that he had gotten a few DUIs and was struggling with drugs and alcohol. I immediately knew it was one of the 12 steps that he wanted to apologize to me for what he had said. I told him not to waste his time and that I had forgiven him and I wasn't interested in the coffee. But back to my story—I even had some old friends who were now working for me just walk out. In fact, even my own brother who also worked for me left and didn't even say a word. I had done a lot for this particular brother and quite frankly employed him when I shouldn't have, and he just walked out. All of the people who left refused to listen and refused to see that these small changes were actually good for them.

I also had another sales agent post on Facebook some pretty graphic and rude comments about me. Now, I usually don't care. After all, people say bad stuff about me all the time because I interact with a whole lot of people through my business. But this agent was a top sales agent, college educated, and a great kid. To be honest, I was shocked and hurt that he would attack me personally considering that he was a smart kid and should have seen why I made the change. I fired him instantly. He didn't say a word to HR when he got his last check and just left. He knew he was wrong. So he didn't make it worse, and he didn't burn the bridge. About a year later, in late 2013, my outbound sales manager asked if I would consider taking him back. I was a little reluctant, but I knew he had just made a mistake. Today, he is my number one sales agent and makes six figures.

Anyway, despite the discontent with my sales staff, we reduced the commission on the larger package by 5 percent and *increased* the commission on the smaller package by 5 percent. Now to put it in perspective, the larger package was roughly $300. By reducing the commission, the salesmen would make $15 less on each package sold. The smaller package was about $150, and the increase there was $7.50. So, net/net, it looked like we were taking money away from them. But what they didn't account for is volume! The smaller packages were much easier to sell, and they were much faster to sell. They were less likely to get returned, and they were actually better for the customer.

The result? What actually happened was the overall commissions paid out went up, we as a company sold a package that was more profitable, and we paid off our debt and stayed in business!

This small change has now led to more stability as a company and given us the ability to continue to hire and grow as a company. We have continued to implement this sales and commission structure across all of our product lines, and it has continued to work. This 5 percent change and increase in sales on one package across all of our products has enabled us to grow our revenue at a rate of 15 percent and 20 percent in 2013 and 2014 while maintaining a healthy profit margin. As a company we are always asking more of ourselves, even just a small bump in productivity; 5 Percent More allows us to expand our business to different markets and grow as a company.

My friend who was working 50 to 70 hours a week, by the way, is now a partner, and we have made some small changes in his business model and things are moving in the right direction. He's still working the hours he was working before, but the small changes we've made have allowed him and his team to become more efficient. One small change we made that has had a dramatic result in productivity, is that we leveraged the technology he already had in his company to make his salespeople more efficient. Once we became partners, my team helped show him and his team how to make some minor changes to things like his sales database that allows his people to accomplish more in less time. When things are difficult and you seem to be doing all that you can and you are looking to make drastic changes in your business, I find it easier many times to make small changes first. The small changes will have the best long-term results.

LOCKER ROOM STORY

I was in the locker room at my gym one day listening to a 20-something kid complain that he was behind in his e-mails—350 of them! He was telling an older gentleman how difficult it was. I almost burst into laughter thinking about how little of a problem 350 e-mails in a day was. Really, you can't handle that? As I write this section on the stationary bike at the gym at 6 PM, this self-proclaimed overworked and overwhelmed guy sits on the bike next to me. What a great opportunity to maximize his time. Right? Well, this same guy who five minutes before was acting like he couldn't breathe because he was being suffocated with e-mails was managing his fantasy football team. So it made me wonder, what if we were more efficient in handling our e-mails or any form of digital communication, or the rest of our lives for that matter? What would that look like to the employee and the employer? What would the employee's life outside of his or her work responsibilities look like? Would they have more free time? How about less stress? Would they be happier? I learned a technique a while back that relates to e-mails. Many of us keep our e-mail open and respond to them as they come in no matter what else we are working on. What happens is, the work we are attempting to complete gets set aside so we can respond to an e-mail. That causes a tremendous loss of productivity, not to mention a whole lot of stress. Instead, try this different method for a week: Close your e-mail while working at your desk, and check it once an hour. This may not work for all office environments, but for most it should. What will happen is, you will actually become more efficient, less stressed, and definitely happier.

JUST TWO AND A HALF DOORS A DAY

I recently had the opportunity to speak at Comcast in Boston in front of their door-to-door sales group. It was such a great opportunity for me, and I had a great time talking about the many concepts in my first book and the 5 Percent More mentality. One of the things I showed them was what just 5 Percent More effort would look like to their bottom line individually. The average salesperson knocked on 50 doors a day, times 5 days a week. That is 250 doors a week, times 50 weeks, for a total of 12,500 doors a year. I challenged them to just knock on 5 Percent More doors a day, which is just an extra 625 doors a year. I made some assumptions for demonstration purposes, but if they just knocked on 5 Percent More doors a day and closed only 5 percent of those people, they would net an additional $6,250 a year on an annual basis. 5 Percent More is only two and a half doors a day on average. Just two and a half doors a day. After my presentation I had several salespeople come up to me to tell me that 5 percent is not only achievable, but easy to do!! You can find that speech at https://www.youtube.com/watch?v=FfmGaOoD6G0.

Now imagine what would happen to Comcast if every sales-person in every division just did 5 Percent More. Do you think their stockholders would be happy? What about the individual sales-people and their families? That kind of money is life changing, on just 5 Percent More effort. The most powerful thing about this example is that just a 5 percent increase in productivity will have between a 10 and a 12 percent increase in their annual salary. Let me repeat: 5 Percent More effort and activity in this example will have roughly a 10 to 12 percent increase in their annual salary. And this does not take into account 5 percent compounded. This assumes that they knock on just two and a half more doors a day.

I was speaking at a business conference recently where people paid as much as $10,000 a seat! My presentation was about the direct response industry and how direct response marketing, if implemented properly, could increase revenue and profitability in virtually any business. Toward the end I discussed the 5 Percent More methodology as it related to making sales and showed an example similar to the one about Comcast. One woman came up to me who is a professional network marketer. She had been in the network marketing business for more than 30 years. She had attended hundreds of trainings and seminars. She was blown away with how simply 5 Percent More would translate to her business and the people in her down line, and was ecstatic to share with them the 5 Percent More way. It is so simple: You talk to a few more people a day who aren't in the business about the business in an attempt to get them in the business. You don't need to talk to every person you see. Why not? Because most people get overwhelmed with the idea of talking to every person they see, and they get anxious. But if we say to just talk to a few a day, just a few more people every day, it is achievable, it is realistic, and it's also sustainable.

MY DAD THE SALES GUY

I talk about my dad in *Ask More, Get More* when explaining increasing one's net worth and exploiting an opportunity. But things actually took a turn for the worse at his job and, even though I am not a big fan of nepotism, I hired my dad in my outbound sales department. Now, before I continue, let me just describe my dad. He is a 64-year-old Italian man who is a product of the sixties. He is hard working and intelligent, but he is also stubborn and does things "his way." So he's a hard-working, stubborn hippie. When I hired him in sales, I explained to him that we had systems in place and there are certain sales techniques that he must learn. His response was just classic my dad: He said, "I do things my own way, I have my own strategies."

Now, I hired my dad because I didn't want him working in the machine shop anymore; he suffers with Bell's palsy and polyneuropathy, and the latter seemed to be getting worse. I told him, "Come in, learn how to sell, but don't worry about making me money." He then responded and told me that he was going to sell, and he was going to make me money but with his "own techniques." Needless to say, he was consistently on the bottom and his techniques didn't work! He was in my office a little while ago and I was telling him about 5 Percent More and discussing with him what just 5 *Percent More* effort and enthusiasm would do for the average person, or just making 5 *Percent More* calls in outbound would look like to his bottom line. He just listened and didn't debate with me about how his system of just talking to people and not actually asking for the sale, or just making a few calls a day, or getting up every ten minutes to smoke a cigarette were the best techniques.

The next day he came to me and asked if I had seen his sales for the previous day, the same day I had explained to him, a non-salesperson in a salesperson's job, the benefits of just 5 *Percent More.* I hadn't looked, but to his surprise—but not mine—he'd had the best day he had ever had. He actually had a 200 percent increase in sales on that day over the prior day.

I asked him what he thought it was that was making him more successful, and he smirked at me and said he was 5 *Percent More* enthusiastic, he made 5 *Percent More* calls, and just gave it 5 *Percent More* effort. I tried to hammer home the point of what had just happened. I said, *"Dad!* With just a little more effort, with just a little more of an upbeat thought process, and with just spending a little more time on the phones, you increased your sales that day by 200 percent!" He proudly announced that he knew it had worked.

Now, here is the challenge: My dad knows that he doesn't have to really try, in fact he probably truly doesn't want to. He has worked his whole life and has taken care of me and now it's my turn to return the favor. But just imagine if you really wanted more and *had* to go get it. Can you believe that just 5 *Percent More* enthusiasm or effort can increase a nonsalesperson's sales? What if you were a skilled salesperson? What if you worked in an assembly line, you think you would increase your net worth by doing things just 5 *Percent More* efficiently? Don't take my word or the science behind my word as truth; try it yourself, and once you see what I have seen, then compound it! It works!

YES, YOU CAN MAKE MORE TIME—AT LEAST 5 PERCENT MORE!

So many people are pressed for time every day. Getting up in the morning, getting in the shower, getting dressed, getting the kids off to school, then the morning commute. Then your workday starts and you are already overwhelmed with stress and anxiety thinking about all the things that need to be accomplished during the day. The pressures of producing in whatever career can be difficult to manage. Most of us are able to work through this chaos and push through the day. But did you accomplish everything you needed to? Are you getting ahead in life in general? Or are you, like most people, aimlessly spinning your wheels dreaming about getting ahead?

So many of us want more, and try to do too much, and try to accomplish too much too fast. What I would like you to try is to just do 5 *Percent More* in whatever it is you are trying to get through every day. By way of example, if you are trying to become more efficient during your day, rather than radically change your daily routine by trying to do more, make small gradual improvements. For instance, if you are a writer and you are always behind the eight ball and find yourself rushing things to meet your deadline, take a look at your routine and find 5 Percent More time in your day to accomplish your main task. Modifying your behavior by just 5 percent is much easier than drastic changes, and scientific research into human nature supports my theory. Doing fewer things just a little better will actually improve your overall productivity.

CHAPTER **15**

5 Percent More Perseverance

When times get tough, the tough give 5 Percent More. Some people at the top appear to be doing things at a pace that is beyond what the average person could even fathom. And they are. But they have compounded on their success. They didn't just get to the level they are at; they worked at it. Whoever you are and whatever your goals and desires are, you will always be challenged and resistance will always be there. Many times, you will fall short of your goals. You will suffer what I call temporary defeats. These are, essentially, lost battles during the war, but you never lose the war unless you surrender. Pushing through just a little bit more than others no matter what level you are at will increase your odds of success dramatically.

That's not typical BS that you read in a lot of other books out there by those self-declared success gurus, many of whom haven't actually ever done anything other than write books about being successful or hold webinars on how to sell their webinars. Quite honestly, most don't have a whole lot of real-world experience. You and I know what it's like to have to juggle life while trying to be successful, and it's not easy. Making ridiculous demands of yourself aimed at becoming a millionaire overnight or changing everything in your life by tomorrow morning won't work. Telling you how I made millions in eight months after sleeping on my sister's couch is not only unrealistic, it is deceptive.

A LITTLE BOY NAMED BILLY

A couple of months ago, I was talking with a very close friend about the 5 Percent More mentality and methodology. The conversation turned to his son in fifth grade and his struggles with his grades. Now, I am very close to my friend's son, too. So my friend asked that I talk with his 10-year-old boy (we will call him Billy) about applying 5 Percent More to his academic life. The boy is a great kid, decent athlete, and not a bad student, but he's just been struggling to break through to achieving solid grades. At the time, he was a D/C student just starting fifth grade. He understood the concepts he was learning, but he had been falling short when it was time to test.

Now, I'm not a teacher or a child psychologist, but I am a parent of a nine-year-old girl. So I gave it a shot. Billy had heard me and his dad talk about business and even this book over the previous several months. When I talked with Billy, I realized and he did too, that what was truly missing from his grades being where they should be was just a little more effort. Just a little more time studying and preparing, and just a little more repetition.

We talked about things like the average number of math problems he had for homework, the average amount of time he read every day, the average amount of time he studied things like science and social studies. Now, I was on the phone with him, so we didn't actually write numbers down together but we talked in general about the 5 Percent More method. But I didn't call it that. I said, "Billy, let's say you have 50 math problems a night for homework. I want you to do two things. I want you to find a way to do three (two and a half would be hard to do) more each night on your own." He said there are tons of websites and apps where he could easily do that. I then said, "I want you to spend about five more minutes during that time double-checking your work." It took him about 30 minutes to do the work. This is more than 5 percent, yes, but still a small number.

Then we moved on to things like science and social studies. Both of those have a lot of memorization involved at this stage in learning. Things like the capital of each state, the key players in the Civil War, or the periodic table. I asked that Billy do the same thing on these subjects, too.

As we were talking, he said, "Mike, this sounds a lot like your book *5% More*." I felt like jumping through the phone, and I said, "Yes! It is!" Then I asked, "Can you do this? Can you spend a little more time? Can you think about your work a little bit more?" He said, "Yes," without hesitation. Now, this was early in the year and Billy was just getting individual test scores back as he started fifth grade. But his dad called me after the first quarter, with Billy on the phone. Billy ended up with a couple of As, a couple of Bs and a C+. Billy had been looking like he would be getting Ds and Cs. Now he is an A/B student. Not because he spends endless hours studying, but just a little bit more time each night. I told Billy that each level or grade he climbs, if he does just a little bit more than what is expected, this will work for him long term. "What is expected," you may say, is somewhat of a moving target. It is something that, at that age, the teachers and parents establish. But for Billy, he is expected to get better-than-average and good grades. How he will achieve that is through a little-known methodology called 5 Percent More.

UNREASONABLE ACTION

I've read some of those books that describe what it takes to become successful as having to employ "unreasonable action" in order to get extraordinary results. These books advocate doing things so out of the ordinary that they describe their own advice as unreasonable. And that's exactly what they are. Trying to go from a mid-level manager to the CEO by taking extreme and unreasonable action is foolhardy and a recipe for failure. I want you to get to the next level, and I want you to do more than others, but getting there doesn't take unreasonable action. It just takes doing a little bit more than others, with consistency.

If really asked, even the self-help gurus I talked about above who advocate for taking ten times more action would agree that it must be sustainable in order to accomplish your goals. Doing things that are so outside of realistic human action right out of the gate doesn't work. You have to make real appraisals of what you are capable of and are likely to actually do.

UNREALISTIC GOALS

Setting what some would believe are lofty goals or stretch goals is not a bad thing. But they cannot be unreasonable and unrealistic; there is a difference. I am one of the few people who will tell you that you must be realistic. Lofty goals, or stretch goals, are the type of goals that seem almost impossible to achieve, but they are not actually impossible. For instance, if you are in your twenties with no prospect of employment and you set a goal at making a million dollars in three years, that is a lofty goal, that would be a stretch goal. But, let's also be realistic and set micro-goals and compound on them. If you want to make a million dollars in three years, that is achievable, it's not unrealistic. A million dollars is a lot of money, but let's figure out the realities of getting there. Let's hit our micro goals each and every day to get to that lofty stretch goal. On the other hand, a totally unrealistic goal would be making that million overnight or in the next 30 days simply by wishing it, or believing you can or should make it happen.

Set your goals as high as you can see. Don't limit your goals. Don't dream about those goals, either, but take realistic actions to achieve those goals. Set them extremely high, higher than what society thinks you should achieve, and get there. But I have seen it time and time again, unrealistic action in an effort to achieve your goals does not work.

Improve upon your goals each day; take small bites of the apple and then bigger bites until your actions become habit. Most research confirms that it takes roughly 60 days for something to become a habit. Going from zero to 60 on day one and trying to sustain that will blow your engine. Improve on your actions a little bit more each day and you will achieve whatever goal you set out to accomplish.

BABY STEPS

The key to success in achieving your goals is to take baby steps. Small changes will yield big results. As I said earlier, and say over and over again, it's so much easier to make small changes and set smaller goals than to make a wholesale change or commitment that can and will shock your mind and body.

A couple of weeks ago, a buddy of mine was at the pool swimming laps. He told me how he was getting to the point of stopping but then told himself to do 5 Percent More. The actual mathematical equivalent of what 5 percent meant is irrelevant. He then went on to swim four more laps. Four more than he had ever done before. Those four more laps represent thousands of more laps over a lifetime and thousands of more calories burned. Those four more laps most likely represent more time on this earth and better health.

So how can you apply this to your life? No matter what the situation is? It's simple. Whatever your task is, whether it be short term or long term, just tell yourself you will just do a little bit more. Then, depending on your goal, you compound it. Each day or week or month, do 5 Percent More than what you previously did, and continue to build on it. Anybody in any situation can do something 5 Percent More, or less even, if it's daily.

I'm a believer in setting big goals and seeing yourself wildly successful. But it doesn't just happen overnight. Setting big goals, I believe, is also a key element to success, but achieving those goals for most must be done in small increments, or micro goals. With micro goals, you will have micro successes that you can compound on. Think big (don't dream big; you know how I feel about dreams), set big goals, but also set smaller goals, work on achieving them each and every day, and move on to the next one.

IT ISN'T ALWAYS EASY

Like I said earlier, and I will repeat it because it's so important. Whoever you are and whatever your goals and desires are, you will always be challenged and resistance will always be there. Many times you will fall short of your goals. You will suffer what I call temporary defeats. These are essentially lost battles during the war, but you never lose the war unless you surrender. Doing things just a little bit more than others no matter what level you are at will increase your odds of success dramatically.

You see, at the end of the day the truth is that most people are fighting a very real battle between the way things are right now in their life, the way they see themselves and their life, and the way they want to be or the life they want to have. Changing all that overnight isn't only improbable, it's probably mentally impossible. Your mind won't even accept such a change.

But you can change little by little and your mind will not only accept that but will adopt the new image and be able to build on it.

To be clear, we aren't talking about being subpar. Doing things subpar will get subpar results. We are talking about doing things

5 Percent More, 5 percent better, 5 percent faster, 5 percent smarter and compounding on it. So what started out as a really minor change will get you major results. But the key is consistency, even when faced with adversity.

Once again I say to you that when you fall short, keep at it and keep working even when it seems like it isn't working. It will. I promise.

SECTION V

5 Percent Compounded

CHAPTER 16

Less Is More

When you look at super successful people, many of them do way more than 5 Percent More than others. These are the people who achieve success that for most is incomprehensible. Wait . . . stop the clock (a phrase coined by Ronnie Mund). Did I just say you can't be the next Steve Jobs? You can't become the next Mark Zuckerberg? No, I said most people can't even begin to see themselves at that level. Reading this book means to me that you want more; you want to be in a position of financial freedom, you want to effectuate change, you want more. I'm just telling you that if you jump in and take what some would call massive action, more times than not you will burn out. Life isn't a sprint. It is a marathon.

MASSIVE AND IMMEDIATE ACTION DOESN'T WORK

I have a guy who works for me in sales. He is one of those guys who is naturally gifted and has the skills that are just part of his DNA. However, he's not my best guy; in fact, in many months he is in the middle to lower half of performance. Every couple of months I give him a pep talk, and his numbers shoot up for a couple weeks. The challenge is, he burns out. He jumps from being an average sales performer to the top performer and burns out. Why is that? Well, I will tell you. Most people are like him. They can go strong for a short period of time but can't maintain. A lot has to do with your brain, as I mentioned in the last chapter.

You see, your brain is like the most amazing computer ever built and it will do what you want it to, but you need to teach and train your brain so that your actions become non-volitional habits. Going from average to great in your brain would be like going from being a weekend warrior at the gym to becoming a professional body builder. It physically can't happen. Your brain will temporarily turn you into that body builder, but until it's trained properly it will burn out. In order for your brain to change to the top-performer mentality, it takes small baby changes to have long-term, wholesale benefits.

Are there exceptions to the rule? Are there people who are outliers and totally destroy my above philosophy? Absolutely. But they are few and far between. I am one of those people who need to make small changes, too. As I type, I'm on the stair climber slowly bringing my body back to the shape I want. I'm slowly getting my diet back in check. Guess what? I'm also making mistakes and falling down. But that is the struggle I talked about earlier. We become a long-term success through the small victories and struggles. No long-term success happens quickly.

TOO FAST AND TOO FURIOUS—HOW NOT TO DO IT!

I started Blue Vase with five people and a quasi-dream/vision. I knew I wanted to be super-successful, I knew I understood the business, and I had a plan. The plan was to slowly, each week, grow our media spends and grow our customer base so that we would have a solid foundation for the future. But being a young entre-preneur, doing anything slowly didn't seem right; it didn't feel right. So we began to grow very fast. We went from five employees our first month to 10, then 20, then 30, and within a year we outgrew our small office—doubling and even tripling our media spend without the proper foresight. The challenge was, since I had started with relatively little money and working capital, we left no room for error.

As we were growing one of our products and contemplating a new office, we got hit with an unexpected challenge. Each week we were literally living hand to mouth, and when the cash came in it went out even faster to pay for the media, the product, salaries, shipping, customer service, and so on. I was personally bouncing my mortgage and car payments every month. As a company, we needed to keep the money coming in so that we could buy products and then resell them. Well, our main product was a dietary supplement that tested positive for E. coli. Fortunately, we hadn't even shipped any yet, but the challenge was, we were out of inventory and it took eight weeks to get more back in.

This was a horrific time. I remember feeling sick to my stomach, as we didn't have the funds to buy more product, and the manufacturer was also telling us he didn't have the funds to cover the new batch. We needed to keep the advertisement on air in order to continue to generate money, but without product we couldn't ship, and things would soon just get out of control.

Fortunately, we came up with a solution. We were able to source the product in half the time and we were able to explain to the customers that the product might be delayed by a week or two. But the point is that if we hadn't been so aggressive, this almost-fatal error would not have happened. The reason the product was shipped to us and had tested positive for E. coli was that the manufacturer was also pushing too hard and moving too fast to keep up with our demand.

We knew as a company we wanted to grow, and we wanted to grow fast, but in all reality we just needed to make small changes in our growth daily that would eventually have led to long-term, sustainable growth. Today, we ship and receive ten times what we did back then, but it was a gradual growth. Week after week, day after day, we have improved our processes just a little bit more, and we have grown a little bit at a time after that initial out-of-control explosion. This small, gradual growth has compounded. It has allowed us to make big moves, but in all reality they were moves that we have been able to make due to our compounded growth.

While we were bootstrapping our business, our technology was not the best, either, but just enough to get us started. Because I was so eager to grow so quickly, a lot of other things started to break. Our phone system was the cheapest we could find and it wasn't really designed to handle the type of calls our advertisements were bringing in. As a result, we had our phone system completely shut down, and we had customers not able to hear us, sales agents not able to hear the customers, and hours without a phone system. The challenge is, when we buy air-time and the 800 number pops up on the screen, customers call. We couldn't just cancel the media once it was already booked. We lost many hundreds of thousands of dollars due to my ambition and drive, but also due to my lack of applying the 5 Percent More growth strategy. Slowly adding more calls, working with the phone system provider to ensure they could handle the growth, and slowly getting better helped us remedy the situation.

Now, we obviously got through these mistakes and challenges, but we would have been much better off if we had just slowly compounded on our growth daily.

TAKE 5 PERCENT LESS

During the tough economic times at my company, I had to ask people to take less, as I alluded to earlier. I reduced the salaries of pretty much every salaried employee. I skipped paychecks and even asked some of my top management to do the same. We all had families, we all had bills to pay, we all had a certain lifestyle to live, but if the company failed, then all of that would have been in jeopardy.

This was not easy to do or to ask, but almost everyone agreed. I lost one person, who happened to be my first HR manager. She was not making a lot of money and I guess even a small reduction in her salary was something she felt she couldn't live with and she was unwilling to make the sacrifice. Now, I don't know her personal story, but I know no one was happy about this, but everyone else stayed. They all stayed because they knew that this small reduction in pay was going to stabilize the company and ensure salaries for the long term. It wasn't like the business was going to end; we just needed to make a few slight adjustments, some of which hurt more than others.

The interesting thing about this woman leaving is, now I have an amazing HR manager, someone I've known for years, and he is now making double what she had been making. At my previous company, when trouble arose, the owners refused to reduce their own salaries, which just helped pour fuel onto the fire in a business that was already up in flames. Sometimes you have to take less now in order to receive more later. None of us have crystal balls, but we all can see into the future by understanding that 5 Percent More, or less in this instance, works.

During this time, I was talking with one of the guys I had pitching one of our products on television. I was not asking him to reduce his cut, because I had already made the adjustments I thought I had to make, and quite frankly he was one of the big reasons why my company was generating revenue. At this time, I was paying him roughly $50,000 a month, and it was growing. He said to me, "Mike, I've been in this business a long time. I have seen companies like yours come and go." He went on to say that this was one of his last products he was pitching and he wanted to reap the benefits long term. I told him I was going to honor the deal we made. At the time of this conversation, I actually owed him $50,000. He then did something that blew my mind. He said, "Mike, forget about the $50,000. I need X amount of dollars to live, and if you can pay that, then just pay me that, and when you can, pay me more. As long as I am getting paid and I can live, I know you will pay me more." Now, the average royalty deal in my business pays out for about three years. I have been paying him weekly, plus bonuses here and there, for seven years and will continue to pay him as long as I am in business. He saw that the small adjustment then would pay out for him long-term into the future. On top of those weekly payments, I paid him that $50,000 as well, because he had already earned it. Small adjustments yield big results.

MORE THAN 5 PERCENT MORE

This whole book is really about showing you how just 5 Percent More effort can get you to where you want to be. Whether it be a better job, a better education, or, the ultimate goal, a better life, 5 Percent More can do that. But what it also can do is give you the ability to go beyond what some would consider too small of a progression. There are many instances in life and in business where you truly have to go beyond just a 5 percent move one way or the other. But, without the proper foundation, a large swing one way or the other has a huge potential for failure. We all hear the inspirational stories of an entrepreneur who went against the grain, took huge risks, mortgaged his life, and became wildly successful. What we don't hear a lot about is all the guys and gals who did the same thing and failed. What 5 Percent More has done for me and my company and can do for you is give you the opportunity to go big when needed because of the foundation that you have built by applying 5 Percent More day in and day out.

Today, I am able to double and triple my media spends when necessary or when the opportunity arises, because we have been able to see our way through the difficulties of growing. We have put processes and systems in place to enable us to grow when it makes sense.

What it also has allowed us to do is expand our reach from Emory Vodka to our next big venture of Daily Fantasy Sports with www.draftdemons.com. Draft Demons is our own Daily Fantasy Sports site where players can join and win real money by picking their best team and play against others. I honestly didn't know much about fantasy sports other than it is a huge growth area online, and I wanted to learn more. Once I looked at the numbers and the growth potential, we launched Draft Demons. We are applying the 5 Percent More mentality and philosophy each and every day and slowly building the foundation just like I have done with other products.

Trust me when I say I want to go big today as I am watching other sites grow at a remarkable pace. But we are not there yet. Our systems are not fully in place, our financing isn't in place, and our marketing plan is still not fully vetted. We could easily go up with our infomercial today and spend money, but it would be foolish and most likely fail. Now, the whole business could fail as well, but even if that were the case, we will mitigate the risk by slowly growing each day so that we will give ourselves the opportunity for long-term, sustainable growth.

We are watching some of the bigger players in this world burn through cash at a remarkable rate, and they are not paying attention to the media dollars being spent. At a conference we attended, one of the largest daily fantasy sports sites said publicly that they didn't know exactly how their media was working but that as a whole it was working. My company, Blue Vase, and our new company, Draft Demons, know how to buy media on a micro and macro level so that when we have the proper financing in place we will know that our media is working and how. The 5 Percent More philosophy has given us the opportunity to take some risks and expand our business, and with each new business we will apply what we know works.

5 PERCENT MORE IS MASSIVE ACTION

We talk about compounding the 5 percent method throughout the book. And, in this chapter and the last one, we warned of over-reaching in your zeal to do too much too fast—and the danger of wanting some massive change too quickly. But I hope you are beginning to realize that each day in which you give 5 Percent More than the previous day, your actions are actually massive: Just not so massive, though, as to cause your brain to short circuit.

When I was general counsel to that network marketing company years ago, we signed a lot of distributors up fast. For those of you who don't know what a networking marketing company is, it's also called an multilevel marketing (MLM). Think of Amway. Now, in MLMs, just like with pretty much every other sales organization, only a small percentage of people have success. As a company we would have trainings, weekend seminars, and motivational speakers all designed to do one thing. That one thing was to motivate you to sell more.

After coming out of every weekend retreat, we would see an increase in sales numbers, and the little dark secret was, most of the sales came from the people in the seminar. *Not* from new people. You know why? Because turning people into salespeople who aren't salespeople and asking them to become a top salesperson overnight doesn't work. So the distributors at the seminar, in order to save face and artificially improve their numbers, bought more product to appear to be in the top.

MLMs put their top people on stage to tell everyone how much money they made and how spectacular those people are. They are spectacular. Some are just outliers and can take massive and immediate action long term, and some can do it short term. But eventually most burn out as the company did. We went from $50 million a year in revenue to out of business the next. Some could blame management, which would be correct. But when you dig deeper, the model of turning people into rock star salespeople overnight wasn't realistic. It's a slow process, and it requires constant trainings in small bursts over time. Companies like Amway and Herbalife and other direct-selling organizations know this. They know and have proven that long-term small growth on an individual level will yield long-term consistent results and produce more outliers than any other method.

On a macro level, if every salesperson at any organization did 5 percent better, the CEO would give his right arm for that. Imagine if every salesperson, every single one in an organization, did 5 Percent More than the previous month? Can you say "companywide bonuses"? Can you say "more money in each person's pockets"? Now imagine compounding this month after month. It can be done!

ONE OR TWO LAST ARGUMENTS FOR LESS IS MORE!

In one study conducted by Dr. Robert Rogers, people were put in front of a computer screen, a letter or number would flash on the screen, and they were asked to indicate if it was a vowel (if a letter) and if it was even (if it was a number). Their reaction times were measured. The more times it switched between a letter flashing and a number flashing, the slower the reaction times got. Thus, even on as simple a task as identifying an even number, multi-tasking slows you way down.[1]

In another study done at the University of Michigan, university students were asked to sort a stack of cards with objects on them in one of four ways: shape, color, shading, or number of objects. As in the previous study, when they were given a stack of cards that needed to be sorted just a single way, they were relatively fast, but as researchers started asking them to sort by color, then shape, then number, and so on, their response times dipped. More significantly, as they added complexity to the sorting (sort in two ways or more) the multitasking lag increased. Therefore, multitasking for simple stuff causes you to slow down, but as the tasks become more confusing that slow-down effect gets even worse.[2]

The effect of multitasking is not just one of efficiency, either. Recent evidence suggests it decreases your very ability to make sound decisions based on self-control even after you are finished what you were doing. Research done at Emory University found that the more multitasking a subject was exposed to in a fixed time period, the less self-control they showed after they were done in a wide variety of tests. The researchers concluded, "Our findings suggest that the benefits of switching mind-sets to accommodate changing situational demands should be weighed against the drawbacks of mind-set switching. The results from five experiments demonstrated that switching mind-sets taxes limited self-regulatory resources.

"Therefore, although activating certain mind-sets can reduce decision and aid judicious decision making, repeatedly switching mind-sets can impair executive functioning and cause self-regulatory failures on subsequent tasks."[3]

What does all this mean? In this day and age, where stimuli are bombarding us every day, with texting, music, television, surfing the Web, and driving, many times all at once, research suggests that doing less more efficiently will help you to accomplish more. You may think that multitasking actually accomplishes more, but many times—and the science proves it—you actually get less done.

At first it might seem somewhat contradictory when the title of this book is 5% *More* to say, "Do less." But it's not. Do 5 Percent More things better, more efficiently. Focus more on the task at hand and you will actually accomplish more.

RINSE YOUR COTTAGE CHEESE

As I sit here and type, my manuscript has been completed, it has been proofed, and it is ready for submission to my publisher. But I couldn't resist the inner voice in me telling me I had to add this one story to help drive home the point that 5 Percent More is not a theory, it is not an idea that "I came up with," as much as it is a principle that I realized. Five Percent More is not about me or "my story." Five Percent More is a real thing, it is a real concept, it is applicable to all people across every cross section of any society, in any place in time.

About a week ago, I picked up the book *Good to Great* by Jim Collins. With millions of copies sold, I was somewhat surprised I had never picked up this book. As I read through the first several chapters, I found myself growing envious of his literary and research skills. This is a great book that delves into what takes companies from good to great. I would have to say that I agree with a majority of what he found. It was a daunting task and difficult to set a baseline for what "great" really is. This wasn't the part that struck a chord with me. It was a little section about cottage cheese and six-time Hawaii Ironman–winner Dave Scott.

As a triathlete, Dave Scott is certainly an elite athlete playing at a different level than weekend warriors; and at his peak he was riding 75 miles on the bike, swimming 20,000 meters, and running 17 miles every day, according to Collins. When I was researching other training routines, Dave Scott's didn't look that out of the ordinary. And though Collins didn't really highlight the training in detail, he did note how Dave Scott rinsed his cottage cheese before he ate it. Rinsing the cottage cheese took off the excess fat, and thus was a small step in the grand scheme of his overall fitness and training. Dave believed it was the little small step of "rinsing the cottage cheese" that gave him the edge against his competition. Can you imagine a tiny step like that making a difference? Seems too small to make a difference, right? But that is exactly the point. It is those small, consistent habits that set us apart. It is those small habits that make some great, while others are just good. So, if you want to win the next triathlon in life, rinse the cottage cheese before you eat it to get the edge.

CHAPTER 17

Change 5 Percent of Your Habits

We all have bad habits. Some might bite their nails, some may eat late at night (two of mine), and others are habitually late for work. Changing your habits can be extremely challenging, especially if they are deep-rooted, long-standing habits. But start by making small changes.

Many behaviorists would violently disagree with me, especially when it comes to addiction. But there are many who would agree. Addiction is something that is different for everybody. But if you drank 5 Percent Less alcohol, smoked 5 Percent Less cigarettes, took 5 Percent Less pain medication, drank 5 Percent Less caffeine, and compounded this day after day, very soon your habits will have changed. Maybe it's not daily; maybe it's weekly.

I was like most people in this country, addicted to caffeine. I would have an iced coffee from Starbucks with a double shot of espresso to start my day. Then I would follow up in the afternoon with a 44-ounce Big Gulp of Diet Coke. As you can imagine, I had sleeping problems, to the point where it was affecting me mentally. Lack of sleep can truly be lethal. So I needed to make a change. I went from an iced coffee with a double shot to just an iced coffee, then a 12-ounce Diet Coke. Then I went to half-caffeinated iced coffee, then a water in the afternoon. Then I stayed there for a little while—about a week. Then, finally, I went to an iced decaffeinated coffee. Yeah, I had minor headaches and it didn't happen over-night. But I took baby steps. Exactly 5 percent? No. But the methodology is the same. Now, as I type I still once in a while have a coffee, or even a soda. But I changed my habits, and my body no longer craves caffeine.

Now, me with my coffee habit doesn't compare to someone with an opiate addiction, but if you start now and reduce 5 percent every day in whatever addiction you may have, your habits will have changed and made kicking whatever bad habit you have a lot easier. Addiction specialists may again violently disagree and even say the words on this page are misinformation and borderline dangerous; however, there is a lot of science behind my words, as you will see.

STOP LYING

Many of you who have gotten to this section of the book may feel like you do more than most: You work harder than other people in your office, you produce good results, but yet you seem to never get ahead. All of this may be true, but you may be missing a few things. Maybe you are, in fact, 5 percent better in many aspects, but not all aspects of your personal and professional life.

A friend of mine is a senior-level sales manager at a Fortune 500 company. He has worked very hard to get where he is today. He wasn't able to go to college so he literally had to do more than everyone else in order to move up. He has been with this company for close to 20 years, and just recently he posted on a social media site that he was feeling unappreciated and that he couldn't believe how his employer was treating him. I called him and asked what happened, and he told me how he was up for a promotion but another manager got it. He explained to me how hard he worked and how dedicated he was. He told me that the other candidate was definitely worthy and was also a hard worker, but my friend felt like he was really a better fit. My friend told me how the other candidate was always happy and upbeat in the office. He told me how much this annoyed him as he told me no one could possibly be that happy and upbeat all the time. He told me how they were at work and being that happy just wasn't realistic. I then told him that is what set him apart and that is why the other guy got the promotion. My friend defended himself and said how he was upbeat too, not all the time, but *most* of the time. The other candidate and my friend were neck and neck for the position, but the other candidate got the position. For a position that requires motivational skills, the other candidate was just a little bit better than my friend.

What I mean by "stop lying" in this section is that if you aren't getting ahead, if you aren't getting results, step back and objectively look at what you are doing and how you are doing it; ask a friend or even a colleague to give you honest feedback and make the subtle changes you need to in order to accomplish your goals.

A LITTLE CHANGE SCIENCE

Progress is impossible without change, and those who cannot change their minds cannot change anything.

—George Bernard Shaw

As a salesperson and a marketer and a lawyer, part of my training has been to learn about what makes people do what they do. How can I convince someone to do something? How can we persuade them to buy something as a company? As a result, I have had the opportunity to study human psychology in an effort to be a better marketer and motivator. I had a sales manager who used to always say, "The only thing that is constant is change."

Most people hate change; they avoid and resist change and get stuck in their ways. That is why so many people fall short of their goals and dreams in life. People think just jumping in and making drastic, sweeping changes will work. Sometimes they do, but most eventually fail. They don't understand that resistance to change is something that is engrained in us physically and mentally. Both are really one and the same. Our physical thoughts are a result of a chemical reaction or hormonal response. So, since we as humans are very resistant to change, I have the unfortunate news to break to you that 5 Percent More is about change. The good news is that it works and they are small changes that will lead to long-term, *big* results.

In order for you to make a change you need to understand that there will be barriers, there will be setbacks, but first you must be willing to make a change in order to achieve your goals. In the late 1970s, two researchers named James Prochaska and Carlo DiClemente introduced the Stages of Change Model. They introduced this model when they were trying to find a solution to help people quit smoking and overcome addiction as a whole, which we have also discussed. In this model they determined that change occurs gradually; early on, people resist, but over time it gets easier and change happens.

Their model identifies six stages of change. The first is *Pre-contemplation*, where basically you haven't even begun to think about making a change. *Contemplation* is when you have begun to think about making a change, but are still a little wary. *Determination* is the stage where you have made up your mind that change is needed. *Action*, then, is when you take steps and have put a plan in place. For most of you, just from reading this book you have leapfrogged ahead to the action phase.

The next stage is *Maintenance*, where you are trying to stay on track but understand you may get off track and it is going to take time. This is where I also see so many people suffer permanent setbacks. If you are dieting and you happen to have an ice cream, it isn't an excuse or a reason to just give up; you have already come so far. Understand that setbacks happen even with the small 5 percent changes, but recognize you haven't lost and won't lose.

Finally, in the *Termination* stage, you have achieved your goal. The Stages of Change Model is still used today to help people understand what needs to be done to kick an addiction or a destructive habit. This model is also being used to help people make the everyday changes they need to make, not just in addiction.

Now that you understand that change really has stages, it is easier to see how small changes make more sense. As I have said earlier and will continue to say throughout, regardless of the science and our understanding of the human psyche, anybody can do anything 5 Percent More, 5 percent better, or 5 percent less.

And remember, again, you are already in the Action stage of change just by reading this book!

QUIT SMOKING IN 20 DAYS

Now, I am not an addiction counselor, nor would I ever claim to be one. And so I am not going to be so bold as to specifically address the many very serious addictions that multitudes of Americans are challenged by, from drugs to alcohol to video games, sex, the Internet, pornography, the list goes on and on in our country and the world. But I can pretty much guarantee that the 5 Percent More approach will help you in dealing with any of those if you take into account the thoughts I shared earlier in this book and in this chapter.

That's because it is my belief that anybody can do anything 5 Percent More or 5 Percent Less and achieve the results they are looking for. The research supports my premise of 5 Percent Less, or tapering off, with respect to addiction to benzodiazepine, a highly addictive drug. In a three-month randomized study published in *The British Journal of Psychiatry*, 180 patients addicted to benzodiazepine were recruited and tapered off their amount of benzodiazepine each week for three months. In this study, the reduction was 25 percent per week with the option to spread out the last two weeks to 12.5 percent. Tapering off over time had a much better success rate versus the control group: Sixty-two percent of the tapering patients were able to kick the habit versus the control group, which saw only a 21 percent quit rate.[1]

I know you are saying, "Well, that's not 5 percent a day." However, in the Buprenorphine tapering schedule and illicit opioid use, this study found that there is no difference between a 28-day tapering schedule and a seven-day schedule when coming off of an opioid replacement drug—meaning that if it is easier for you to gradually taper off over time you will have the same success rate. In fact, most clinicians prefer a longer, gradual taper (quoted in the study). The study did conclude that there is no benefit to a long-term taper, but if you have seen drug addiction like I have, a gradual, longer taper seems easier on the addicts.[2]

However, when it comes to specific addictions, I am going to spend some time talking about cigarette addiction. And that's because smoking kills more Americans than guns, car accidents, prescription drugs, and illicit drug use combined.[3]

Some experts say that quitting smoking is harder than quitting heroin. I've actually visited several addiction treatment centers and all of them have recovering addicts out in front of the facility puffing on cigarettes like it was their last one. Doesn't that seem odd to you? Practically all addiction centers allow smoking. Why?

Well, I asked the director of a facility in Oklahoma and he said, "If we didn't allow smoking, we would never get people to quit the 'real' drug." My grandmother and great-grandfather died of emphysema and lung cancer, respectively. My mother smokes and my father, despite a recent heart attack, still smokes even though he kicked a cocaine addiction in the nineties. They have both tried to quit several times, so this section I have written is for them.

If you smoke or know someone who smokes, do you think reducing the amount by 5 percent each day is achievable? One cigarette? Of course it is. Let's assume you smoke a pack a day; that is 20 cigarettes. Reducing that amount by just 5 percent a day, you will be smoke-free in less than a month. To help you quit, think about this fact: for every cigarette you smoke, you reduce your life expectancy by 11 minutes.[4]

Now let's assume you smoke every day. You are reducing your time on the planet by 54 days every year. Smoke for six years and you will die a year earlier than your counterpart nonsmoker. Five Percent Less for only 20 days will give you more time on this planet with your loved ones. It's that simple. Anybody, including you, can do 5 Percent More, or in this case 5 Percent Less.

What about the cost of smoking? In a study recently published on www.wallethub.com, you could not only save your life but increase your net worth. If you were to quit smoking versus a life-long habit, you will increase your net worth by close to $2 million. From reduced earnings to the cost of tobacco, you can become a millionaire if you are a smoker right now. Reduce by just 5 percent a day and you will live longer and earn more. The following chart shows you the cost per state.

Overall Rank	State	Total Cost per Smoker	Tobacco Cost per Smoker (Rank)	Health Care Cost per Smoker (Rank)	Income Loss per Smoker (Rank)	Other Costs per Smoker (Rank)
1	South Carolina	$1,097,690	$786,346(1)	$121,270(8)	$179,410(9)	$10,665(30)
2	West Virginia	$1,105,977	$803,863(2)	$127,950(10)	$166,586(3)	$7,577(1)
3	Kentucky	$1,115,619	$823,327(3)	$110,321(2)	$173,710(4)	$8,261(3)
4	Mississippi	$1,150,702	$870,041(10)	$113,451(4)	$155,395(1)	$11,815(39)
5	Georgia	$1,153,516	$831,113(5)	$116,403(5)	$195,403(20)	$10,597(29)
6	Tennessee	$1,166,693	$866,148(9)	$113,137(3)	$178,284(6)	$9,124(11)
7	Alabama	$1,176,633	$870,041(10)	$120,938(7)	$174,449(5)	$11,206(34)
8	Missouri	$1,177,230	$825,274(4)	$151,417(29)	$190,291(15)	$10,248(25)
9	North Carolina	$1,186,790	$862,255(8)	$128,205(11)	$186,440(11)	$9,890(21)
10	Louisiana	$1,207,594	$897,291(13)	$117,784(6)	$178,932(8)	$13,586(47)
11	Idaho	$1,209,154	$883,666(12)	$128,737(12)	$187,725(14)	$9,027(8)
12	Arkansas	$1,215,647	$934,272(17)	$106,863(1)	$165,065(2)	$9,447(17)
13	North Dakota	$1,220,666	$842,791(6)	$143,610(22)	$224,074(32)	$10,191(24)
14	Virginia	$1,247,844	$848,631(7)	$132,121(13)	$257,268(43)	$9,824(19)

Overall Rank	State	Total Cost per Smoker	Tobacco Cost per Smoker (Rank)	Health Care Cost per Smoker (Rank)	Income Loss per Smoker (Rank)	Other Costs per Smoker (Rank)
15	Oklahoma	$1,255,719	$938,165(18)	$121,334(9)	$184,298(10)	$11,922(40)
16	Indiana	$1,274,264	$932,326(16)	$137,831(18)	$195,183(19)	$8,925(5)
17	Nebraska	$1,281,059	$903,130(14)	$157,339(32)	$209,590(26)	$11,000(32)
18	Wyoming	$1,293,459	$905,076(15)	$145,780(24)	$233,364(35)	$9,238(14)
19	Kansas	$1,319,229	$967,361(19)	$133,263(14)	$207,297(25)	$11,308(35)
20	New Mexico	$1,320,560	$988,772(23)	$143,449(21)	$178,488(7)	$9,851(20)
21	Nevada	$1,325,116	$973,200(21)	$135,602(15)	$207,154(24)	$9,160(12)
22	Oregon	$1,348,224	$986,825(22)	$150,145(26)	$202,038(23)	$9,216(13)
23	Colorado	$1,352,541	$967,361(19)	$137,654(17)	$236,199(37)	$11,327(36)
24	Ohio	$1,357,236	$1,016,021(27)	$138,475(19)	$194,951(17)	$7,790(2)
25	Montana	$1,370,191	$1,021,860(29)	$150,823(27)	$187,480(13)	$10,028(22)
26	Florida	$1,372,374	$996,557(24)	$171,447(36)	$187,158(12)	$17,212(51)
27	Iowa	$1,380,804	$1,017,968(28)	$142,830(20)	$210,744(28)	$9,262(15)
28	Utah	$1,391,897	$1,002,396(25)	$136,360(16)	$238,929(38)	$14,212(48)

(continued)

Overall Rank	State	Total Cost per Smoker	Tobacco Cost per Smoker (Rank)	Health Care Cost per Smoker (Rank)	Income Loss per Smoker (Rank)	Other Costs per Smoker (Rank)
29	Pennsylvania	$1,436,403	$1,060,788(31)	$154,672(31)	$211,968(30)	$8,974(7)
30	Minnesota	$1,437,858	$1,008,236(26)	$173,930(37)	$243,947(42)	$11,745(38)
31	Texas	$1,448,653	$1,074,413(33)	$149,000(25)	$209,610(27)	$15,629(50)
32	South Dakota	$1,452,902	$1,088,038(34)	$154,315(30)	$201,275(22)	$9,275(16)
33	Michigan	$1,492,182	$1,144,484(35)	$143,672(23)	$194,995(18)	$9,031(9)
34	Delaware	$1,492,717	$1,047,164(30)	$194,254(44)	$242,348(40)	$8,952(6)
35	California	$1,508,790	$1,062,735(32)	$188,368(41)	$243,352(41)	$14,336(49)
36	Arizona	$1,527,427	$1,167,840(39)	$151,197(28)	$198,068(21)	$10,322(26)
37	Illinois	$1,549,069	$1,152,269(36)	$158,720(33)	$227,660(34)	$10,421(27)
38	Maine	$1,580,359	$1,185,358(40)	$192,545(42)	$193,412(16)	$9,043(10)
39	Wisconsin	$1,605,164	$1,220,393(41)	$164,702(34)	$211,213(29)	$8,855(4)
40	Maryland	$1,651,906	$1,160,055(37)	$185,701(39)	$295,168(51)	$10,982(31)
41	New Hampshire	$1,654,680	$1,160,055(37)	$219,555(48)	$263,931(44)	$11,140(33)
42	Washington	$1,670,552	$1,253,482(42)	$167,874(35)	$239,055(39)	$10,141(23)

Overall Rank	State	Total Cost per Smoker	Tobacco Cost per Smoker (Rank)	Health Care Cost per Smoker (Rank)	Income Loss per Smoker (Rank)	Other Costs per Smoker (Rank)
43	Vermont	$1,741,661	$1,298,249(44)	$213,097(47)	$219,720(31)	$10,595(28)
44	District of Columbia	$1,747,869	$1,261,268(43)	$201,847(45)	$273,156(47)	$11,599(37)
45	Hawaii	$1,853,787	$1,383,891(46)	$185,972(40)	$270,537(46)	$13,387(46)
46	New Jersey	$1,874,155	$1,381,944(45)	$193,312(43)	$286,922(49)	$11,977(41)
47	Rhode Island	$1,945,724	$1,481,211(49)	$224,902(49)	$227,154(33)	$12,458(43)
48	Massachusetts	$1,979,050	$1,457,854(47)	$238,937(50)	$269,831(45)	$12,429(42)
49	New York	$1,982,856	$1,527,924(50)	$208,467(46)	$233,894(36)	$12,570(44)
50	Connecticut	$1,992,690	$1,461,747(48)	$239,866(51)	$277,970(48)	$13,106(45)
51	Alaska	$2,032,916	$1,553,228(51)	$182,575(38)	$287,546(50)	$9,566(18)

Source: http://wallethub.com/edu/the-financial-cost-of-smoking-by-state/9520.

CHAPTER 18

This Changes Everything—It's a Lot Bigger Than 5 Percent

NO ONE WILL OUTWORK ME

To the fans and everybody in Gator Nation, I'm sorry. I'm extremely sorry. We were hoping for an undefeated season. That was my goal, something Florida has never done here. I promise you one thing, a lot of good will come out of this. You will never see any player in the entire country play as hard as I will play the rest of the season. You will never see someone push the rest of the team as hard as I will push everybody the rest of the season. You will never see a team play harder than we will the rest of the season. God bless.

—TIM TEBOW'S PROMISE SPEECH

In 2008, after a heart-breaking loss, Tim Tebow, the then-quarterback of the Florida Gators, gave a post-game speech to the press that has further immortalized his work ethic. In that speech, he told the press that no player and no team would outwork the Florida Gators that season. Everyone knows that working hard in most circumstances will yield results. The speech was heartfelt and inspiring, but what a lot of the general public missed was that

Tim Tebow, the leader of a Division 1 top-level football program, recognized that they hadn't worked hard enough to set them apart and get them to the level that they wanted to be at. It was a tear-jerking and inspiring speech, but what he was saying was that loss was really a result of being outworked. Just slightly outworked, as the loss was by only one point. But it was one point that ruined the possibility of an undefeated season. The Gators went on to win every other game that season, including the National Championship, but that one day and the preparation leading up to it was just not enough to win and they lost by one point.

How can you relate to elite athletes and CEOs at the top of their game? Those business leaders almost certainly outwork a CEO of a small business. Tiger Woods definitely outworks your local golf pro. Seven-figure salespeople outwork the average door-to-door salesperson. Or do they?

The answer is that the 5 Percent More mentality works at each level you climb. Tim Tebow and every other quarterback at the Division 1 level all work hard; Tim Tebow worked just a little bit harder than the rest. Now I know what you are thinking: Natural ability is something that we can't account for. Natural ability helps and can set people apart but it gets you only so far. Well, Tim Tebow is not naturally gifted; he is short, doesn't have the strongest arm, and was prone to making mistakes. But he was a Heisman Trophy winner, won two national college championships, and had a short but successful run in the NFL. Why? Because he worked just a little bit harder than his counterparts. His NFL story hasn't fully been written, but many coaches and analysts, whether they are fans of his skills or not, all agree that having Tim Tebow on their team is a good thing.

Once you get to the next level or you are on your way up, work just a little bit harder each and every day. Not 100 percent more, just 5 Percent More, and you will excel at each and every level of your career and in life.

RECOGNIZE WHAT LEVEL YOU ARE AT

In life there is a hierarchy, there are levels that we have to achieve day in and day out to get what we want and go where we want to go. Tim Tebow, Tiger Woods, Tom Brady, and every other professional athlete worked just a little bit harder than their competition at each level. Their slight edge is what got them to the next level. That top salesperson or the elite real estate broker who is listing multimillion-dollar properties appears to outwork the guy who is selling trailer homes. But that isn't necessarily the case, and in many instances is not the case at all.

The more effort you put in at each level, regardless of the level you are at, the greater your chances of achieving success at that level and allowing you to make it to the next level.

But you must recognize that you must climb to the top of each level in order to make it to the top. Bypassing or skipping levels rarely yields long-term positive results. That top salesperson in your organization, the head nurse at your hospital, the chief information officer at your company didn't just wake up and achieve that level. They worked hard, and they did it by slightly outworking their competition.

To illustrate what I mean by different levels, if you are a freshman in college, in order to graduate and go on to law school, you need to work hard. But to ensure success you must work just a little bit harder than those who are at your level (freshmen trying to eventually get into law school). If your goal is to just barely graduate and hope to land a job, then you probably don't have to work 5 Percent More than the rest of your class. But if you want to graduate with honors and give yourself a chance to get into law school or graduate school, recognize what level you are at (in this example, you are a freshman in college) and what level you want to achieve (graduate school or law school), and work 5 Percent More than all of those at the same level looking to achieve similar goals.

Now, this advice actually applies to you even if you don't want to achieve great things. You see, in college many students just go through the motions, doing just enough to get by. If you are one of those and want to just barely get by, then to ensure that you just barely get by, I would say to you, work 5 Percent More than the other slackers and you will just barely make it. But if you are looking to do something with your life and you are one of the students who work hard, who care about their future and are looking to achieve more, like getting into law school, then look at your peers who have the same goals and do just a little bit more than them.

What will that do? Well, first of all, it will guarantee success and it will appear to all those below you, those who are just aimlessly wandering around through life, as if you are working so much harder than them, but in all reality you are working just a little bit harder than those at the *level* in which you want to achieve.

Now go backward or down and think about those people who appear miserable and always in a rut, and take a close look at what they are doing. Some may be working three jobs and appear to be "working hard," but when you look closely, you will see at least at each level they are at that they are just working to get by.

If you are one of those people who think you work hard, look at those around you on the level you are at and give 5 Percent More: 5 Percent More effort, 5 Percent More enthusiasm, 5 Percent More of everything and anything that will set you apart from the rest of the pack. It sounds crazy if you really are working three jobs, and raising a family, to work harder, but you can. Step back and ask yourself, "Can I do more?" Can you do just a little bit more to set yourself apart, to get you that raise that you need to save a little bit of money or help you get the car your family needs, or to help provide healthier food for your family? You actually can.

When you are exhausted and feel like you have given it your all, remember this section of the book and give it just a little bit more. That small extra effort is going to pay off more than you think. It may help you get to the next level and get you on the path you want to be on.

CAN'T SKIP A LEVEL . . . OR CAN YOU?

The interesting thing you will find is that when you perform slightly better than your counterparts and then make it to the next level, you may find yourself way ahead of those at that next level. In many instances, from school to work or even in social circles, there are people who shouldn't be there. Maybe their parents own the company, maybe a friend gave them the job, or maybe the management is not properly managing the staff and is promoting the wrong people.

I have a friend who is a classic hard worker, someone who always seems to be busy, but he never seems to climb to the next level. We talked about why and discovered that, despite what she thought, she was not very efficient at her job and had a lot of activity but not accomplishment. She was always at work before others and there when everyone left, but she wasn't getting ahead. When we identified that her valuable final product (VFP) or her work output weren't where they needed to be, things changed for her dramatically. We slightly changed her activity to focus more on accomplishment and she actually started working fewer hours and eventually got a promotion.

Others at her company were baffled. Someone who always seemed to be working hard started working less and then got a promotion? How was it possible? She looked at those around her in her department, identified what they were doing, cut out some unnecessary activities that were not work-related, and excelled. But that wasn't even the best part of the story. When she got a promotion and climbed to the next level of management, she found that those at that level were not nearly as efficient as she was; they didn't appear to be working very hard at all. It is the classic story of how middle management actually can hurt a company because they become content and their environment is stagnant. My friend recognized this and she rose to the top of her new middle management job and she now holds the title of vice president. It won't surprise me if her next title is CEO.

STOP DREAMING

I recently was counseling an artist friend of mine about his plans. He told me he will achieve all of his dreams and that he was a dreamer by nature. Then he said to me, "Every artist is a dreamer." I said all of them are broke. The successful ones have vision. They don't dream. They have a vision and set goals and objectives.

By this point in the book, you know pretty much my position on dreaming. I tell people all the time that dreams are for sleeping and goals are for achieving. Dreams are just that. They are a fictitious made-up reality in your brain that is anything but reality on this planet. So I say stop dreaming big and have big vision, and visualize yourself becoming what you want to be. But dreaming, by the nature of the act, will not get you to where you want to be. Set goals, and objectives within those goals.

Let me give you a recent example of one of my goals. My company had just launched Emory Vodka, an ultra-premium vodka, in a very saturated vodka market. If I were a dreamer I would say it will be the No. 1 vodka worldwide in a couple years. But instead, I have a vision of Emory Vodka being one of the top ultra-premium vodkas in the world in five years, and I have goals and objectives as well as a plan to hit those goals and objectives.

Here are my first goals for this venture. As I type, it is May 1, 2015. My goal is to have the vodka distributed in four states by the end of the summer. My objective is to build brand awareness and sell 1,000 cases before the end of fall. It's a pretty realistic and achievable goal. But you will also notice it is a small and achievable one, one that I will build on and use this small momentum to make the next step. We have an integrated marketing plan on how to do this as well.

So first I have my vision, then I have my goal, and within my goal I have an objective. The last one is key. What am I going to accomplish? I am going to sell product while building brand awareness.

And those aren't just strategies that work in the vodka business, but in every business, even those occupations that are often thought of as more artistic, like writing. Remember the writer on my staff? He sets a goal, works toward it and if he hits it he gets just a little bit more out of himself, increasing what? His net worth to the company. It's the small things that make him and many employees valuable to my company.

So stop dreaming and start goal setting. Goal setting will allow you to accomplish those bigger plans that seem like a dream. Don't lose your vision, just put a plan in action by setting small daily goals to accomplish what you desire.

DON'T GIVE UP

> No man ever achieved worthwhile success who did not, at one time or another, find himself with at least one foot hanging well over the brink of failure.
>
> —Napoleon Hill

About 30 years ago, three guys in Southern California started a technology company. There was one clear leader in the group. He was the visionary, the salesperson, and the one who didn't know the four-letter word "quit." His partners were a little wary, but stuck around to watch the company literally come from a garage to a real company. But one partner couldn't do it anymore; he couldn't handle the stress. He lasted only 12 days. He was nervous and his fear clouded his judgment to just hang in there a little bit more. So he sold his stock for $800 in 1976 back to the other two partners. By 1980, the company had over $100 million in revenue, and today that company you may have heard of is Apple Computers, which is valued at an estimated $700 billion in 2015—yes, with a "B"!! That man is Ronald Gerald Wayne, and in his own words he said, "I had every belief [Apple] would be successful, but I didn't know when, what I'd have to give up or sacrifice to get there, or how long it would take to achieve that success."[1]

Now, in all fairness, he has also gone on to say that he believed it was the right decision for him at the time, but if he had just hung in there a little longer and also given a little more effort by helping Steve Jobs and Steve Wozniak, his share would be worth an amount in the hundreds of millions of dollars.

In 2008, two college buddies decided they wanted to start a band. One was the lead singer and the other was the drummer. They recruited a couple of other guys, and the drummer's wife sang backup and played the keyboard. From 2008 to 2011, they actually released a couple of records and had a solid fan base in the state of Utah where they resided, and even signed a contract with Interscope Records. But for the most part they did not achieve much acclaim for their music. Shortly after signing with Interscope, the drummer decided that he had put enough effort in and it was time for him and his wife to leave the band. Almost immediately after they left, the band began to climb the charts, with one record in 2012 debuting No. 2 on the Billboard charts. Many were songs the drummer had performed on. In 2013, the band's second single on that 2012 record went on to sell over 3 million copies, the band won a Grammy, and the album is multiplatinum.

That band is Imagine Dragons, and they are continuing to have success with more songs and their music can be heard on the radio, in commercials, and even in video games. The drummer, Andrew Tolman, asked to come back to the band, but as you can imagine they didn't take him back. If he had just put in a little more effort, a little more time, he would still be in the band.

Lots of people from all walks of life work hard, but what separates good from great is really just the small percentage of time and effort needed to get you to the next level. So many people quit just before not only achieving their goals, but many times just before becoming wildly successful. What separates the Usain Bolts from the rest is just a fraction of a second. Do just a little bit more, for a little bit longer than others, and you will not only reach your goals, but achieve success!

CHAPTER 19

A Line in the Sand—What If Everyone Did This?

After doing everything I could to get into law school, one of my first experiences was somewhat bizarre. There were about 200 of us in the night program and we were all sitting in an old auditorium in the historic town of Boston. It was hot, we were all anxious, and I was personally overwhelmed with anxiety. A few professors got up and told us what to expect, and gave us the realistic view of what law school was really going to be like. They told us things like close to 40 percent of us would not graduate, that we would eventually alienate our friends, and then they dropped the bomb. They asked how many of us were married.

Now, this was the night program, so all of us worked. Most if not all of the class raised their hands when asked if we were married. Then the professor said, "Ninety percent of you will end up divorced." I was shocked and appalled. How could they be so sure? The professor went on to say that not only is law school demanding, but it changes you as a person, and then the profession of practicing law is even more difficult and most marriages do not survive. Law school requires all of your time. Then, when you actually graduate, studying for the bar requires more than all of your time. You are studying when you are sleeping, showering, or using the bathroom. Then, if you are lucky enough to pass the bar exam *and* get a job as a lawyer, sleep is not an option and all waking hours you are thinking about the law. In other words, something has to give. When I say you have to give 5 Percent More at your job, or with your family, it can be done. But if there literally are not enough hours in the day, something does have to give. For me, the professor was right, and I ultimately chose my profession over my marriage.

I have learned, however, that it can be done and can be balanced. I have a very good friend who is a partner at a very large law firm in Boston. He graduated from a small school in the Northeast. That's how he describes Harvard. He has been married for more than 20 years, has two beautiful daughters, and is in a great marriage. I asked him how he does it. This is the key: He and his wife sat down and discussed his career and how much time is involved and how competitive the practice of law is. When I was discussing with him my book at 11 PM one night while he was still in the office, he said to me, "Mike, in what I do, the difference between life and death or winning and losing, many times is just 5 Percent More effort on my part." Now again, he and I were talking about his relationship, management of time, and my book, so this was on his mind. But he said that he and his wife knew that, in order to actually make their marriage work, there had to be some sacrifices.

They knew that opposing counsel was also in the office late at night plugging away and crafting their argument. What I am saying here is that 5 Percent More does, in fact, apply to every aspect of your life, but you need to assess the situation, clearly define the goal, and, if other people's lives are involved, they have to understand what it takes to get to the next level. Like anything in life, sacrifices have to be made in order to reach a goal, but if everyone understands the plan, it is a lot easier to not only achieve the goal, but keep the other aspects of your life on track. I didn't have the discussion my friend did, and when it did get brought up it was too late. I was gone too much and hyperfocused on my career. Five Percent More is a powerful tool, but you also need to understand how to apply it with balance.

This book, like my last, is not an autobiography and is not designed to shine a light on how great I am or how great my company is. It is completely the opposite. I have made a lot of mistakes, I used to dream, I spun my wheels, I have been broke. But I have also seen a lot, I have met a lot of successful people, and, yes, I have achieved a lot of success. But I also want to accomplish so much more. Writing 5% *More* has reminded me how well it actually works. I am far from perfect, I am always working to get better, and I also struggle. But what gets me through the struggles are those baby steps, those small action plans, those mini victories. Those victories offset the temporary defeats that also come along the way.

Blue Vase, through not only a 5 Percent More mentality, has gone from a small company with five people to an internationally recognized company that has generated tens of millions of sales, year in and year out. We want BIG things, and myself of all people want them now, but we know as a company that the small incremental changes are what have enabled us to withstand the tough economic times, and grow at a rate much greater than 5 percent. We have been recognized in *Inc.* magazine as one of the fast-growing companies for the past three years with amazing growth. Last year, our three-year growth was 74 percent!

We run our business at a level that any Fortune 500 business does. We are accountable for our actions, and we always want more. Remember the geometric progression principle? My first week in business, we did $25,000 in sales; we now do close to $100,000 a day in revenue, sometimes more. This success comes from many things, but we have asked for just a little bit more in each department, from each employee. *Ask More, Get More* helped change our culture at Blue Vase, but 5 Percent More has changed our business, so that everyone at every position at the company can relate. Each person knows they can do 5 Percent More; they know they can do just a little bit better each day, each week, month, and year; and that turns a small, fledgling company into a multimillion-dollar enterprise.

Now, in full disclosure, I want to reiterate what I said above, that writing *5% More* reminded me of what we were essentially already doing at the company. It wasn't a term we used day in and day out, but it's what we applied. It happened organically for many reasons, one being the fact that I know what it's like to be asked to do more at every position in my company. The other major reason is, throughout those years when we were financially strapped, we couldn't go bigger; it wasn't an option. So we methodically, with relative caution and a little bit of risk, grew the business every day.

As a businessperson and entrepreneur through and through, I want to go big on so many things, but going big too fast doesn't allow you to work out the kinks, it doesn't allow you to adjust your plan like I discussed earlier. And, of course, we learned that lesson when we tried to grow too fast.

But forget about the past now and let me give you another contemporary example. When we test a new advertisement, we spend about $5,000 the first week, then maybe $7,000, then $10,000, $15,000, and so on. When we get to about the $15,000 mark, I instinctively want to press the gas pedal and go hard and fast. In all honestly I still do, and nowadays we can afford to. But almost every single time when we do we start to see breakage, and the media doesn't perform as well as it did when we slowly make small increases.

The reason why is simple. When we increase too fast, we are not able to see everything clearly and we aren't able to adjust every aspect of the business accordingly in order to maximize profitability from the ads. Can we do it? Can we grow that way? Absolutely; but the incremental growth of 5 percent, whether it be a day or a week or a month, has always seemed to work better for us.

THE NEXT STEP

I recently listened to a speech by former Navy SEAL Marcus Luttrell in front of University of Alabama's football team. He is the inspiration behind the movie *Lone Survivor*, which depicts what four Navy SEALs went through in Afghanistan. It is beyond comprehension what our men and women do for us every day. Marcus described how he had been shot several times, and suffered broken bones all over his body, his brother was dead, and he was paralyzed from the waist down. He had lain there knowing he was dying but had to do something about his situation. So he literally drew a line in the sand and dragged himself to where his feet touched the line, then he did it again and again and again for seven miles until he was taken in by villagers and eventually saved.

In life, many of us are faced with what seems like insurmountable adversity, whether it be something basic like an overwhelming workload, to climbing the proverbial corporate ladder, to overcoming physical challenges. But, if we take on those challenges a little bit at a time, we will eventually get to where we want to go.

Marcus Luttrell was a highly trained Navy SEAL. He was a part of the most elite military fraternity in all the world. He was mentally trained to overcome and handle adversity beyond belief. Very few of us will ever be in a situation like the one he was in. But in that speech, he taught us and the Alabama football team that it is just about pushing forward even if it is a yard at a time no matter how battered and bruised you are.

And anyone can move forward just a few inches, or yards, at a time. Whatever the challenge is, taking on just 5 Percent More at a time, you will be amazed how much you really can accomplish.

NEXT LEVEL STUFF

Okay, now you understand that 5 Percent More can work for you in achieving your goals. Maybe by now you have gotten that raise you wanted, you have begun to become more physically fit, you are reading more to your kids, and so on, because the 5 Percent More mentality has become a habit. So now what? How do you become the next Steve Jobs, Bill Gates, Warren Buffett? I'll bet you think I'm going to tell you that you have to do more than 5 Percent More. Wrong. I'm going to tell you to do exactly what you have already done. You have to have vision and a goal. If your vision and goal is to be at the pinnacle of business success, then keep applying the 5 Percent More mentality day in and day out to that end. It works. How do I know? I've seen it work personally and through other people's experiences.

Consider the Olympic or professional athlete or the top-level CEO. They are just doing a little more than their competitors. As you climb each level, 5 Percent More works. Remember that little known mathematical theory of geometric progression? It works at any level. But sustained growth and success must be gradual. Continue to do 5 Percent More as you climb each level and understand you can always climb higher.

Throughout the book we have talked about recognizing the level you are at, and applying the principles in this book at each level. You can use these principles to excel at any level. But ultimately you can move up a level by excelling at each one. And that's my ultimate goal for myself and for you.

People often ask me if I will ever be satisfied. The answer is yes. But it does not mean I do not want more, it does not mean I am going to stop growing personally and professionally. If you set a goal and you get there by applying a 5 Percent More mentality, then set a new goal. It is important to reevaluate your goals every so often to make sure your plan is being effectuated. My company continues to build on its successes and learn from its defeats. We are exploring other business opportunities and creating more for ourselves.

Okay, so now you know anybody can do 5 Percent More of practically anything. You've realized that it's almost too easy, and you are right, it is. By now you have already incorporated 5 Percent More into many aspects of your life.

So here is the next step. Do More.

If you would like some more information about me, my webinars, or seminars, you can visit my website at www.michael-alden.com. You can also find me on Instagram @MikeAlden2012, Twitter at MikeAlden2012, SnapChat at MikeAlden2012, and Facebook at www.facebook.com/TheAldenReport.

Notes

CHAPTER FOUR   MAKE 5 PERCENT MORE MONEY

1. www.census.gov/quickfacts/table/PST045214/27097/embed/accessible.
2. www.cnpp.usda.gov/sites/default/files/usda_food_plans_cost_of_food/CostofFoodJul2014.pdf.
3. www.vermonttreasurer.gov/sites/treasurer/files/pdf/literacy/InfoSheet DoublingPenny.pdf.

CHAPTER FIVE   BE 5 PERCENT SMARTER

1. https://financialaid.uoregon.edu/uo_presidential_scholarship.
2. www.usnews.com/news/articles/2014/02/11/study-income-gap-between-young-college-and-high-school-grads-widens; www.pewsocialtrends.org/2014/02/11/the-rising-cost-of-not-going-to-college.
3. https://law.ucla.edu/about-ucla-law/school-facts.
4. www.ets.org/s/gre/pdf/gre_guide.pdf.

CHAPTER SIX   BE 5 PERCENT STRONGER AND FASTER

1. www.iaaf.org/athletes/jamaica/usain-bolt-184599#progression.
2. Martin McDonagh et al. "Adaptive Response of Mammalian Skeletal Muscle to Exercise with High Loads." *European Journal of Applied Physiology.* 52:139–155, 1984; Martin Gibala et al. "Myofibrillar Disruption Following Acute Concentric and Eccentric Resistance Exercise in Strength-Trained Men." *Canadian Journal of Physiology and Pharmacology* 78 (2000):656–661.

CHAPTER SEVEN   BE 5 PERCENT HEALTHIER

1. www.sciencedirect.com/science/article/pii/S1053810010000681.
2. http://online.liebertpub.com/doi/abs/10.1089/acm.2010.0142.
3. http://newsroom.heart.org/news/meditation-may-reduce-death-heart-240647.
4. http://news.uic.edu/massage-therapy-beneficial-after-injury-exercise.
5. https://nccih.nih.gov/research/results/spotlight/020812.htm.
6. http://medicalxpress.com/news/2014–05-underscores-benefits-clinical-massage-therapy.html.

CHAPTER TWELVE   READING 5 PERCENT
MORE TO OUR CHILDREN

1. Judy A. Theriot, Sofia M. Franco, Barbara A. Sisson et al. "The Impact of Early Literacy Guidance on Language Skills of 3-Year-Olds." *Clinical Pediatrics* 42 (March 2003):165–72.
2. Betty Hart and Todd R. Risley, *Meaningful Differences in the Everyday Experiences of Young American Children* (1995), 132.
3. Ibid., 176.
4. Ibid. (preface).

CHAPTER THIRTEEN   5 PERCENT MORE REVENUE

1. www.forbes.com/global/2000/1127/0324130a.html.

CHAPTER SIXTEEN   LESS IS MORE

1. Robert D. Rogers and Stephen Monsell, "Costs of a Predictable Switch between Simple Cognitive Tasks," *Journal of Experimental Psychology: General* 124, no. 2 (June 1995): 207–231.
2. http://umich.edu/~bcalab/documents/RubinsteinMeyerEvans2001.pdf.
3. http://goizueta.emory.edu/profiles/documents/publications_working_papers/hamilton/switchingmindsets_obhdp_2011.pdf.

CHAPTER SEVENTEEN CHANGE 5 PERCENT OF YOUR HABITS

1. http://m.bjp.rcpsych.org/content/182/6/498.full.pdf.
2. www.ncbi.nlm.nih.gov/pmc/articles/PMC3150159.
3. www.cdc.gov/nchs/fastats/homicide.htm.
4. http://www.ncbi.nlm.nih.gov/pmc/articles/PMC1117323.

CHAPTER EIGHTEEN THIS CHANGES EVERYTHING—IT'S A LOT BIGGER THAN 5 PERCENT

1. https://www.facebook.com/RonGWayne/posts/370073493010333.

Index